Illuminating The Darkness

A Fresh and Effective Solution to Depression, Stress, and Anxiety

Noel Dear

Abide With Him Publishing

ISBN: 978-0-9850692-0-9

Published by Abide With Him Publishers,
Newark, Ohio

Subject Heading: CHRISTIAN LIVING

1 2 3 4 5   16 15 14 13 12

To my four beautiful girls...

Donna—my amazing wife and best friend
Hannah, Emily, and Rae—my delightful daughters

With special thanks to my editors...

George Lambert
Ray Wagner
Warren Way

CONTENTS

FOREWORD

Noel Dear (pronounced "knoll" as in a grassy knoll. Not the way we would pronounce the word "noel" during the Christmas season) has been the senior pastor of my home church for the last six and a half years. I'm honored to have him as a personal friend. Our families have spent many hours together and shared many meals together. One of our recurrent topics of conversation has centered around the intersection of our chosen professions. I am a family medicine trained physician who currently treats opiate addicts almost exclusively. During our conversations I've threatened to someday write a book concerning the poor decisions we make in our lives. Life is difficult enough the way it is, but most of us make decisions that make our lives even more difficult. We pay for those decisions not only financially, but with poor health, broken relationships, limited success, etc.

Our own decisions often lead to unhealthy levels of stress, anxiety and depression. Estimated costs of these problems are in the range of 42-53 billion dollars annually. Studies have been conducted to examine the efficacy of treating depression with exercise. An article from the January 2005 American Journal of Preventive Medicine concludes that aerobic exercise at a level consistent with public health recommendations is an effective treatment for major depressive disorder.

A study published in American Family Physician's January 1, 2006 issue evaluated the efficacy of Cognitive Therapy for treatment of depression. Cognitive therapy is a treatment process that enables patients to identify and correct false beliefs that lead to negative moods and behaviors. Studies have shown that cognitive therapy is an effective treatment for depression. Most physicians don't have the time and many don't have the desire to take the time to have these important conversations with their patients. Perhaps more regrettable most people don't take the time to develop close relationships with wise people. We all need people in our lives who, with only genuine concern, will say to us, " I love you. What you are doing, thinking, etc. is wrong and here is why..."

Noel Dear is a scholar. He knows how to study (an important skill we do not all possess) and cherishes his study time. He has done all of us a favor by completing this important book. The information in "Illuminating The Darkness" is sound. From his years as a Bible scholar and teaching pastor he has put together an easy to digest, biblically fact based exploration of depression, stress and anxiety.

Solid information exists making our belief that Jesus of Nazareth was indeed who he claimed to be (i.e. the son of God) a reasonable one. Christianity is not just a religion. It is not a club we have chosen to join. It is a comprehensive explanation of all reality—the reality of how the world works. Pastor Dear has extracted the biblical principles dealing with depression, stress and anxiety making them clear and easy to understand. Medical research has shown exercise and cognitive therapy to be an effective prescription for the treatment of these problems. Biblical truth is the prescription from the creator of the universe for these problems. I beg of you, do not dismiss sound biblical advice with intentional disregard. These disorders take so much away from not only the one who suffers from them, but from their loved ones as well. You will greatly benefit from the reading and understanding of "Illuminating The Darkness."

Eric Chico, DO
Granville, OH
February 2012

CHAPTER 1

AM I NORMAL

Depression, stress, and anxiety have many faces. They affect us in very different ways. For some they come as a slow, dull malaise that creeps into a person's mind and sets up camp. For others, it is more sporadic. However, when they hit, they knock you down. Sometimes they travel alone; sometimes in a pack; sometimes they bring friends like anger, bitterness, jealousy, and fatigue.

Are you suffering with one of these? How many friends and family are depressed, stressed, or consumed with worry?

The words are really hard to define. Definitions of depression range from a relatively mild sounding explanation like:

"a state of low mood and aversion to activity"

To something much more ominous sounding like:

> *"a chronic medical illness that usually requires long-term treatment, like diabetes or high blood pressure, and that may cause people to lose interest in activities that once were pleasurable, experience overeating or loss of appetite, or problems concentrating, and may cause people to contemplate or attempt suicide"*

In addition to those broadly different characterizations, you probably have your own definition. Thus, while it may be hard to define depression, what is not hard is knowing you are suffering. There is no pain like the pain of depression.

The Survey Says...

In an attempt to get a sense of how people would describe depression, I sent one hundred random people in my address book an email asking them to describe the pain of depression in a sentence or two. Here are some of the things I heard back most often. (By the way, no one emailed back and said they were unfamiliar with the pain of depression.)

- Depression is a sad, hopeless, nothing matters, feeling that you seem powerless to get out of.

- I believe depression is the inability to see beyond your pain. It would be like looking ahead and seeing a brick wall instead of a path.

- Sadness and gloominess, self-pity and total discouragement, hopelessness...

- Depression to me feels like heavy weights are attached to my body, my feelings, and my emotions.

Some of the most common words in the replies I received were: hopelessness, drained, heaviness, deep-hole, and sadness. Does any of this sound familiar? Would you use some of the same words in your description of the pain of depression? I imagine so.

Is This Normal?

Is this normal? Is this just the way life has to be? Are these unavoidable emotional struggles, at least for some people? Those are very important questions, especially if you have been struggling with one or more of these for a long while.

So let us look at the concept of normal. There are two ways to measure normal.

The first way is to look at what normally happens in life. By that measure depression, stress, and anxiety are very normal. In fact, they seem to be almost universal.

If you want to see how *normal* these three states of mind have become in our culture, just look at our language. See how many of these phrases you can complete.

- I've had it up to ...
- I am sick and ...
- I am worried to ...

- I am about to blow my ...
- I am a bundle of ...
- I am so angry I am blue in the ...
- I am stuck between a rock and a ...
- They are driving me up the ...
- I got up on the wrong side of the ...
- If it's not one thing, it's ...
- I feel like resigning from the human ...

How many ways do we know how to say we are depressed, anxious, or stressed?

Statistics tell us that in any six-month period, four out of every ten people in America suffer from depression, stress, or anxiety, and they suffer seriously enough that it interferes with their normal routine and responsibilities. This makes these characteristics more normal than blue eyes or blond hair.

normal \ nôr'məl \ conforming to a type, standard, or regular pattern

—Merriam-Webster

But are they really normal? Not necessarily. There is another way to measure normal. We can compare our emotional health to a standard or a benchmark. Let me explain.

When my wife or I take one of our daughters to the pediatrician for her annual check-up, the doctor will measure and weigh her. He will measure her height, the circumference of her head, her reflexes, and so on. He does this in an attempt to see if she is normal. So how does the good doctor know what normal is? Does he compare her measurements to those of the other kids in the waiting room? No. He looks to a chart that represents the standard. The chart tells him what normal is. The chart tells him what the circumference of her head should be. It tells him how tall she should be.

If the doctor has a chart that indicates what is normal for a person's physical measurements, where is the chart we can ⁎ hold our lives against to see if we are normal in a mental or emotional sense? I suggest the standard is found in the Bible. (And you will see why I suggest this later in this book.) The Bible sets the bar for what our normal mental and emotional condition should be or at least could be.

When we measure depression, stress, and anxiety against the standard seen in Scripture, we see that while they are widespread, they are not normal. They may be the way many or most live today, but they are not the way we were made to live.

So what does this mean?

The Bible shows us that there is hope. There is a better way to live! Look at some of what the Bible says.

Always *be full of joy* in the Lord.

Philippians 4:4 NLT, *italics mine*

When troubles come your way, consider it an *opportunity for great joy.*

James 1:2 NLT, *italics mine*

Let the *peace* that comes from Christ rule in your hearts.

Colossians 3:15 NLT, *italics mine*

I am leaving you with a gift—*peace of mind and heart*. And the peace I give isn't like the peace the world gives. So *don't be troubled or afraid.*

John 14:27 NLT, *italics mine*

May the Lord of peace himself always give you *his peace* no matter what happens.

2 Thessalonians 3:16 NLT, *italics mine*

Don't worry about anything; instead, pray about everything. Tell God what you need, and thank him for all he has done. Then *you will experience God's peace*, which exceeds anything we can understand. *His peace will guard your hearts and minds* as you live in Christ Jesus.

Philippians 4:6–7 NLT, *italics mine*

The Holy Spirit produces this kind of fruit in our lives: love, joy, peace, patience, kindness, goodness, faithfulness, gentleness, and self-control.

Galatians 5:22–23, NLT

Therefore, the Bible gives us a picture of what life should look like, and *on-going depression, stress, and anxiety are not a part of that life.* This means there is hope; our lives do not have to be plagued with depression, stress, or anxiety. There is a way to overcome these struggles.

Are Depression, Stress and Anxiety Sin?

If depression, stress, and anxiety are not normal (at least compared to the standard given in Scripture), then this prompts another question. Are they sinful?

Why would we even ask that question? Many people who suffer from emotional battles bristle at the suggestion that the Bible says we can live differently because, in their minds, this means the Bible must be saying it is their own fault. Because of this, some people get defensive when they read Scripture that says "always be full of joy;" and in doing so they reject the one true source of real freedom and recovery.

I attended a Christian writer's conference recently where I shared with other writers some of what you will read in this book. Although most were encouraging, one fellow participant, who heard the premise of this book, became so irate she went to the leaders of the conference and asked them to make me leave. She said she could not sit in the same room with someone who believes the Bible offers a real way out of depression, stress, and anxiety.

I do not know her story, although I have counseled with enough people who share her disposition to make a good guess. I imagine she believed any suggestion that a person can overcome depression using biblical wisdom is also a suggestion that emotional pain is the direct result of personal sin. I felt sad for her. She will likely live out her days in her own emotional hell while relief, the relief I will show you in the remainder of this book, is close at hand.

So, is it a sin to feel depressed, stressed, or anxious?

The simple answer is, no. You feel the way you feel. If a door slams on my finger, it will hurt. It would be foolish for someone to tell me my finger should not be hurting. I feel what I feel. Always be wary of someone who tells you that you should or should not feel a certain way.

It is important to know that being depressed, stressed, or anxious could involve sin, just like anything else in life could. (If I keep slamming the door on my finger, for example, eventually I may have to take some responsibility.) However, to say, feeling stressed equals sin is wrong, and the Bible makes this crystal clear.

Emotionally Challenged Bible Heroes

Jesus' time in the Garden of Gethsemane the night before his crucifixion is an excellent example of this. He knew what the next twenty-four hours held for him. He knew about the physical pain and anguish of the cross. He knew about the shame. He knew about the crushing weight he would bear as he took the blame for sins he did not commit. And he was, by any contemporary definition of the word, stressed-out! Read this:

> My soul is crushed with grief to the point of death. Stay here and keep watch with me. So he prayed more fervently, and he was in such agony of spirit that his sweat fell to the ground like great drops of blood.
>
> Mark 14:34; Luke 22:44 NLT

Through no fault of his own, Jesus was stressed. His stress was stress without sin.

There is also precedent in the Bible for some pretty godly people being very depressed, even depressed to the point of wanting to die.

Have you ever heard of a man named Moses? He was leading the entire nation of Israel on a long hike and a forty-year camping trip. The people were uncomfortable and complaining, and Moses took the brunt of their displeasure. He had finally had enough.

> Moses said to the LORD, "Why are you treating me, your servant, so harshly? Have mercy on me! What did I do to deserve the burden of all these people? Did I give birth to them? Did I bring them into the world? Why did you tell me to carry them in my arms like a mother carries a nursing baby? How can I carry them to the land you swore to give their ancestors? Where am I supposed to get meat for all these people? They keep whining to me, saying, 'Give us meat to eat!' I can't carry all these people by myself! The load is far too heavy! If this is how you intend to treat me, just go ahead and kill me. Do me a favor and spare me this misery!"
>
> Numbers 11:11–15 NLT

Have you ever felt like that? Have you ever said, "I can't handle all of this alone?" Have you ever felt so down that you have prayed, "Oh Lord, please just kill me right now?" If you have, then you are in good company. Moses did the same.

Elijah, the famous Old Testament prophet, was suffering from anxiety (he feared for his life) and fatigue. Listen to what he said:

He went on alone into the wilderness, traveling all day.
He sat down under a solitary broom tree and prayed
that he might die. "I have had enough, LORD," he said.
"Take my life, for I am no better than my ancestors who
have already died."

1 Kings 19:4 NLT

What about Jonah? Do you know about Jonah and the
big fish? Near the end of the account, we read in the book of
Jonah that he feels like nothing is ever going to go his way.
He says:

Just kill me now, LORD! I'd rather be dead than alive if
what I predicted will not happen.

Jonah 4:3 NLT

The Bible also includes a strong theme of lament and
sorrow. It even encourages us to be broken over our sins
and sinful lives.

Let there be tears for what you have done. Let there be
sorrow and deep grief. Let there be sadness instead of
laughter, and gloom instead of joy.

James 4:9 NLT

So if someone says, "If you love the Lord you will be
happy all the time," they are just wrong. What they have
done is to oversimplify something so much they turn it on
its head and make it wrong. (And a statement like that hurts
people much more than it helps them.)

What if I said, "Tall people are men?" That is true much of the time, but it does not mean there are not some short men and some very tall women. It also does not define what is meant by tall. Tall compared to whom? If a woman teaches a class of second graders, she will most assuredly be the tallest person in the classroom, but she also is most assuredly not a man!

There is some correlation between our walk with the Lord and happiness or emotional health, but exactly how that works is not as simple as saying, "Just love God more and you will feel fine." In fact, our normal understanding of feelings is a big part of the problem, as we will see in the next chapter.

Why are you cast down, O my soul, and why are you in turmoil within me?
—PSALM 42:5

Earlier I mentioned asking one hundred random people in my email address book to describe the pain of depression. I told them I was studying what the Bible said about depression. Several of them replied rather defensively, demanding that I not say, "If you just love God and pray then your depression will go away." Well, I am not saying that, and it would be wrong to do so.

So what am I saying? What should we take from all of this? There is hope! There is a better life possible for those who continually struggle with depression, stress, and anxiety!

Because I am a local church pastor, many people share their stories with me when life gets hard. I have learned quite a few things through just listening. One is that life is hard for everyone from time to time. No one escapes the difficulties of life. However, I have also learned that different people have different *normals* in life.

For some people, normal is depression and anxiety and discouragement and strife. Those people do not bounce back very well. They hit emotional walls like a half-deflated basketball, no bounce back. Others, however, seem to live on a different plane. They are not necessarily healthier or wealthier, nor are they in a better place in life, but they are emotionally strong. Sometimes, life hits them hard, but they bounce back to their *normal* in short order.

You can be in the second group. You can have a new normal in your life. There is hope! I have seen the principles shared in this book revolutionize the emotional health of many people. My prayer is that they will do the same for you.

VINE DRESSING

1. How common are feelings of depression, stress, and anxiety among your friends and family?

   Very strong in me.

2. How does it make you feel to know there were times when even the greatest Bible heroes suffered from mental and emotional anguish?

   Not alone,

3. While the Bible acknowledges the presence of depression, stress, and anxiety even in the most spiritual people, it paints a picture of a different kind of "normal" living. How far is your "normal" from the way the Bible says life can be?

   Very far. I don't have a close walk w/ the Lord. or as close as I should have

4. What do you think the correlation might be between a person's walk with the Lord and their emotional health?

   Positive Strong correlation Spirit filling

CHAPTER 2

THE PROBLEM ISN'T WHAT YOU THINK

There are two key principles that will redefine what you think of depression, stress, and anxiety. These principles will be critical to understanding and benefiting from the solution we will discover in later chapters. These principles are not difficult to understand, but because they will likely be very new to you, it is important that we investigate them closely.

Symptoms or Causes?

When you ask someone struggling with depression or stress to describe the problem, he or she will most likely begin to speak about how he or she feels. We see negative feelings as the problem.

- I feel tired.
- I feel a sense of hopelessness.
- I feel stressed out.
- I feel lonely.
- I feel nervous.
- I feel frustrated.
- I feel sad.

In our way of viewing things, we think our main problem is the way we feel. When we say we are depressed, we are describing how we feel. Depression may involve emotional feelings like discouragement, hopelessness, or loneliness; it may involve physical feelings like fatigue or pain; it may involve spiritual feelings like guilt or bitterness. The feelings of depression are real, and they can be very debilitating.

Therefore, we say things like...

- My problem is depression.
- I must overcome my depression.
- Do you have a pill that treats depression?

People write books titled...

- The Depression Cure
- Surviving Depression & Anxiety and Making the Most of Bad Genes
- Overcoming Depression One Step At A Time

The same thing is true with stress and anxiety. We think those are our problems.

As it turns out, when we look more closely at things, most of the time, the pain or the bad feelings are not the real problem. Nine times out of ten emotional pain, physical pain, and even spiritual pain or discouragement are not what is causing the misery!

I know that sounds absurd. The reason you are reading this book is because you have a problem or you know someone with a problem with the pain of depression or stress or anxiety. How could pain not be a problem?

Well, I did not say it was not *a* problem, only that it is usually not *the* problem.

Imagine you are a physician, and I am your patient. I come to see you because of severe pain in my left foot. I take off my shoe and you look at my badly bruised foot. It is swollen on the top from the ankle all of the way to the toes. It is obvious that it must be very painful. I ask if you think there is anything you can do. You ask me, "How did this happen?" I explain that I go bowling every day, and when my hands get slippery, I often drop my bowling ball on my foot. It happens six or eight times a day.

What would your suggestion be as my medical doctor? Would you just prescribe some pills to help my throbbing pain? Would you give me some anti-inflammatory medicine to deal with the swelling?

No! Not first anyway. You would begin by telling me to stop dropping the bowling ball on my foot! Perhaps I need to bowl with some gloves, or maybe a bowling lesson or two would help. Maybe I should take up a less dangerous sport such as carpet golf or badminton.

My problem is not chiefly the pain in my foot. My problem is that I keep dropping a fifteen-pound bowling ball on my foot. The pain is not so much a problem as it is an indicator of a problem. The pain tells me it is potentially dangerous to drop bowling balls on my foot over and over again. When I see it in that way, I can see that often pain is not only *not* the problem, but it is a benefit; it is an advantage. Sounds odd, but it is true.

While none of us welcomes or enjoys pain, I imagine you can think of a thousand ways pain is a good thing. Are you glad it hurts when you put your hand on a hot pan or a hot stove? If it did not, you could easily cause damage to your hand that would never heal!

Are you glad appendicitis hurts? If your appendix could become infected and rupture without your knowing it and going to the hospital for treatment, it would be a fatal infec-

Pain is not really a problem as much as it is the indicator of a problem.

tion nearly every time. Pain is a good thing when it is an indicator of a problem that needs to be fixed or treated.

Putting on your doctor hat again, how would you suggest a person treat a broken arm? I have never broken my arm, but I understand it can be very painful.

There are three courses of action you can take to treat the patient with a painfully broken arm: You can treat the symptom, which is severe pain; you can treat the cause, a broken arm; or you can treat both the symptom and the cause.

A competent doctor wouldn't seek to treat the patient with painkillers alone. The proficient doctor wouldn't just give the patient a year's supply of high potency pills and say, "If it still hurts at the end of the year, come back and see me."

No. A skillful doctor would treat the cause of the pain. He would treat the problem, not just the symptom. Sure, he or she would likely give the patient some pain medicine to assist with the temporary pain, but the doctor would never treat the pain in lieu of treating the problem.

Therefore, the first lesson we should learn is that depression, stress, and anxiety are really symptoms of some deeper problem. Depression is not the problem; it is the symptom of the problem. Stress is not the problem; it is the symptom of the problem.

This is an important lesson. Once we understand that these are symptoms, then we can begin to dig down, and find and fix the real cause.

Too Much of the Bad Or Not Enough Of the Good?

We must make a second distinction before we can find help. Are these emotional struggles the result of too much of something bad in our lives or are they the result of not enough of something good in our lives? Are these struggles ailments or deficiencies? This may seem like a complicated and unimportant question, but in fact it is key to really understanding the depression and anxiety people struggle with.

To find the answer and understand how important this is we need to do a little activity.

What are some of the words people use to describe negative emotional feelings or experiences? It is not hard to think of a few:

- Depression
- Strife
- Irritability
- Stress
- Anxiety
- Worry
- Anger
- Being Out-Of-Control

We could write down many more, but these cover the biggest categories. No one wants his or her life described by any of these words. We universally fear these things.

If these are the emotional problems, then what are the opposites? If these are the negative feelings and experiences we dread, what are the positive feelings we desire? It is extremely helpful for us to be able to identify not only the emotional hardships we face, but also identify the emotional health we long for.

If you pull out a map to determine the best driving route for a trip, you cannot do anything until you know two things. First, you have to know your current location. Then you must know where you want to end up. Only then can you plan your journey.

So if the starting place is depression, strife, irritability, stress, anxiety, worry, anger, and being out-of-control, then where do we want to end up? What are the opposites?

Let us look at a few of these one at a time.

Depression

While depression can take on many different forms, a general definition would include times of sadness, gloom and hopelessness that are not necessarily tied to the circumstances of life. Often when someone is depressed, it takes more than a little bit of good news to lift the pain. Depression can set-in when difficult times come, and it can remain once the difficulties pass. While many depressed people can point to something they view as the ongoing source of their depression, many depressed people cannot.

What is the opposite of depression? I think the best word to describe the opposite emotion would be *joy*. Joy is a happiness that is not impacted by the circumstances of life. Some people seem to have a kind of happiness that can survive almost any bad news they receive. This is joy! We all know people who have joy even when life is very difficult.

Therefore, depression and joy are opposites. This is important. Do not forget it.

Strife

This one is easy. No one wants his or her most important relationships characterized as filled with strife. So what do we want our relationships characterized by? *Love!*

Sure, there are other words we could use: trust, kindness, openness... However, the best umbrella term for all of these would be love. Therefore, the opposite of strife is love.

Stress

Stress is a universal struggle. Rare is the person who can truly say his life is completely free from stress. So what is its opposite? What would we like to replace the stress we face in life?

Peace! Most people would give an arm and a leg for some peace, a peaceful day, a peaceful night, a peaceful meeting, a peaceful marriage, a peaceful job. We want peace in our finances, in our schedules, in our relationships.

Down with stress. Bring on *peace*.

Anxiety/Worry

Everyone knows what it is like to have a lump in the back of the throat because you are fearful about what may happen next. All of us have lain awake at night thinking about what bad thing might happen the next day or the next week. Worry is definitely a negative emotional feeling. If we reversed worry, what would we have? We would have *patience*.

We are patient when we can wait, without fear or restlessness, for the future to arrive. Patience is not always having confidence that things will turn out fine, but it is the quality that allows us to handle things one day at a time. Patience allows us to sleep at night even when there is great uncertainty about the future. Patience allows us to enjoy a day with our family even while we dread an upcoming meeting or confrontation at work.

Out-of-Control

Sometimes emotions like stress, depression, strife, and worry can lead us to the place where we are out of control. Maybe we are out of control in the reckless words we say. Maybe we are out of control in our spending or our eating or in the abuse of alcohol or drugs.

If we could trade in our out-of-control temperament, with what should we be looking to replace it? *Self-control.* Self-control is what we need for every area of our lives. We want to be able to be disciplined, strong, and reliable.

Light versus Darkness

Why is it helpful to know the opposites of the emotional struggles we face?

This is the start of a completely new way to look at stress, strife, depression, anxiety, and an out-of-control temperament. You will need to keep an open mind to understand this, but this new understanding will be the beginning of a breakthrough.

The question we must answer is: Are emotional struggles like depression actual illnesses or are they the result of a deficiency of emotional health? Another way to ask the question is this: Are we depressed because there is something wrong with us or are we depressed because there is something not right with us?

In no way am I suggesting depression is not real. I am simply trying to get to the heart of the problem. If my stomach hurts, it could be because I have an infection or food poisoning (meaning something is wrong), or it could be because I have not had anything to eat in two days (meaning something is not right).

Perhaps a better way to understand this is to compare light and darkness. The office I am working in right now is brightly lit. It is brightly lit because there are three overhead light fixtures and a few lamps all shining light into the room. Now, how would I make the room dark? Would I turn on some dark fixtures? Would I use some sort of machine to shine darkness into the room? No, of course not. I would simply turn off the lights.

Darkness is the absence of light. It is still real. It can still cause great problems. Darkness cannot be ignored. This is why we have lamps, streetlights, headlights, flashlights, etc. However, *darkness is not the presence of something bad, it is the absence of something good.*

For it is you who light my lamp; the LORD my God lightens my darkness.

—PSALM 18:28

Could it be that what we commonly call depression is actually the absence of joy? Could it be that what we commonly call stress is really the absence of peace?

This is exactly the case! (And as we will see in the next few chapters, this is what the Bible teaches.)

Sure, stress is a real problem, just as not eating food for a week would be a real problem. If your body is weak from a lack of food over the past week, the best way to treat the problem is to introduce some *eating* into your schedule. If your body is emotionally weak due to stress, perhaps the best way to treat the issue is to introduce some *peace* into your life.

Anxious? You need *patience*.

Depressed? You need *joy.*

Someone will say, "But I've always heard that depression is caused by an imbalance of chemicals in the body." Hold that thought; we will get to that soon enough. For now, let us consider that at least for some depression, there may be another fundamental cause. People generally *feel* depressed because they are not *filled* with joy.

From what we have learned in this chapter, do you see now why most treatments for depression, stress, and anxiety are so ineffective in the long term? We have learned two reasons in this chapter:

- These flawed approaches are often treating the symptoms instead of the causes.

- These so-called remedies are trying to chase away the darkness instead of turning on the light.

What we need is a way to target the real cause of these emotional struggles and supply the needed ingredients for emotional health and strength.

VINE DRESSING

1. How is the pain of depression or anxiety similar to back pain or abdominal pain? What is the purpose of all pain?

   It can physically hurt & tell us something is wrong.

2. How can pain be a good thing?

   tells us something is wrong

3. There are many "treatments" available for all kinds of mental illness. In your view, do most of those treatments address the root cause of the issue or do they simply address the symptoms?

   Counceling w/ meds shows more improvement
   I have added a spiritual layer

4. No one wants to be depressed. So what exactly do people want to feel? In your view, what is the best replacement for depression? What is the best replacement for stress? For anxiety?

   Joy, Peace, Patience

5. For most readers of this book, there has been some previous experience with depression "remedies." Would you characterize those "remedies" as chasing away the darkness or turning on the light?

   Chasing the darkness, or

CHAPTER 3

THE BIG DISCOVERY

I magine how you would feel if you were digging in your back yard to plant a garden and you stumbled across a shiny yellow rock that turned out to be an outcropping of the largest vein of gold discovered in the last 50 years? Eureka! Your financial problems would be solved now that you have access to an endless supply of wealth.

Let me show you the emotional health equivalent to discovering the largest vein of gold in America. I am not suggesting that you will never have another emotional difficulty in life, but I also do not want to underestimate the power of the discovery I am about to share. While this may seem simple to begin with, this profound truth can change your life.

There are two very interesting Bible verses buried deep within a seldom read book in the New Testament that speak volumes as to how we can overcome depression, stress, and anxiety. Read closely.

> The fruit of the Spirit is love, joy, peace, patience, kindness, goodness, faithfulness, gentleness, self-control; against such things there is no law.
>
> Galatians 5:22-23

Picture a beautiful basket of fruit. In the basket are nine varieties: joy, peace, patience, kindness, goodness, faithfulness, gentleness, and self-control. Think about each fruit. Is that something desirable? Would you like your life characterized by that fruit. What if the words used to describe your life were joy, or peace, or self-control?

Now imagine, and I know this is odd, that your life is represented by a fruit basket. What kind of fruit do you have in your basket? What kinds of fruit would your friends or your spouse describe as filling your basket?

When we look closely at these nine fruits, we quickly see that this is a perfect description of emotional health. Every attribute of emotional health is covered. Nothing is omitted. Everything that is covered is desirable!

Visualize two contrasting people. Let's imagine they are both ladies. One is fruit-filled as described by the two verses we just read, and the other is barren, meaning her life is devoid of the fruit of the Spirit.

> **Person A:** *She is loving. She cares for people, and gets along with those around her. There is no strife in her life. She is joyful. She loves life and it shows. She is peaceful when others would be stressed-out. She is fearless. She is patient and*

worry-free. She is kind, calm and good. She is trustworthy and dependable. She is humble, and she is disciplined.

Person B: *She is angry and everyone knows it. She is in constant conflict even with those closest to her. She is depressed, stressed out, and worried. She dreads the future and believes for some unknown reason the world is out to get her. She is unkind, stingy, and selfish. She cannot be relied on. On top of all of this, she is arrogant and obnoxious, lazy and disorganized.*

Which of these two people would you like to have as a friend? Is that a hard choice? How would you like to be married to someone like person A? How would you like to be married to someone like person B? When you look at it from this perspective, figuring out this fruit-of-the-Spirit thing might not just help your emotional health; it might also drastically improve your married life!

Therefore, the fruit of the Spirit clearly describes what it would be like to have complete emotional health. This is the gold standard. This is the destination everyone wants to get to in his or her emotional health. It is not that we just want to numb our depression and hammer down our stress. No. We want joy! We want peace! We want the fruit of the Spirit!

> *Figuring out this fruit-of-the-Spirit thing might not just help your emotional health; it might also drastically improve your married life.*

The end of the Bible passage says, "Against such there is no law." This tells us something we already know: No one is against these things! These fruits are not traits that just spiritual people or just religious people desire. These fruits correspond to what every person desires. No one can deny that a person characterized by these nine fruits will have a happier life. Moreover, no one can deny that this person will be a much better person to live around than the person who is lacking some or all of these.

These nine fruits are the answer to our biggest emotional health problems. What if you could buy these in pill form? Do you think you could sell some joy pills? What about peace and patience pills? How many people who struggle with diets and exercise would be interested in buying a self-control pill? Can you think of someone in your life to whom you would like to give a very large bottle of kindness-goodness-gentleness pills?

Every good gift and every perfect gift is from above, coming down from the Father of lights
—JAMES 1:17

In chapter two, we learned that emotional struggles like depression or stress are actually caused by a deficit of some good things in life. Here we see what those good things are. They are the fruit of the Spirit. Just like darkness fades when the lights come on, so depression will fade when the fruit of joy buds in our lives. How do we overcome stress? We grow some peace.

This sounds pretty simple. Maybe it sounds too simple. However, even if you are skeptical, give an honest answer to these questions: Doesn't the fruit of the Spirit describe what we all really desire in life? Wouldn't you do almost anything to have your life characterized by these fruits?

So the million dollar question is, "Where do we get this fruit?"

The Source of the Fruit

The verses in Galatians not only tell us the nature of the fruit but also tell us the secret of the source of the fruit. Read them again, and see if you can find it.

> The fruit *of* the Spirit is love, joy, peace, patience, kindness, goodness, faithfulness, gentleness, self-control; against such things there is no law.
>
> Galatians 5:22-23, italics mine

The key word is the third word in the passage, the word *"of."* This is the fruit *of* the Spirit. *Of* tells us the source of the fruit. In this passage, *of* means *from*. If we were to say, "These are the children of the king," we would be saying that these are the king's children. Their source is the king. Therefore, we learn from these verses that this fruit comes from the Spirit, meaning the Spirit of God. The source of this fruit is God!

Notice how the source of the fruit is even more clearly described in a different Bible translation:

> The Holy Spirit produces this kind of fruit in our lives: love, joy, peace, patience, kindness, goodness, faithfulness, gentleness, and self-control. There is no law against these things!
>
> Galatians 5:22–23 NLT

The passage says, "The Holy Spirit produces this kind of fruit in our lives!" You cannot get this fruit anywhere else. You cannot get it from a pill. You cannot get it from another person with whom you have a relationship. You cannot get it through some exercise or technique. It does not come from better lighting or ventilation. It does not come from garlic, St. Johns Wort, or fish oil. You cannot get it from a book, including this one!

You can only get it from the Spirit of God. Of course, there are some things you can and should do to ensure you receive this from God, and this is the point of this book. But first we must remember that the fruit we seek is only found in and from the Spirit of God.

Good News or Bad News

Is it good or bad news that the only source of the fruit is God? It is bad news if you are searching for emotional health from other sources. As I read articles and books on overcoming depression, stress, and anxiety, I see how many of the so-called experts lament how unsuccessful their standard treatments are from a long-term perspective. I notice how seldom their treatments even attempt to address the underlying causes of the problems. It seems many of the approaches boil down to modern and sophisticated versions of the "take two aspirin and call me in the morning" approach of old. These approaches give remedies that simply numb the pain for a period of time but never bring real, lasting emotional health.

I talk with many people who have been battling depression for decades. It seems they have tried everything. They have read books, talked with counselors, taken pills, changed diets, changed jobs, changed friends, changed spouses, and nothing has given them lasting victory over their melancholy.

Therefore, the fact that the only source of the fruit is God is bad news for those who are searching elsewhere. However, it is good news if you are frustrated with your past attempts to overcome depression, stress, and anxiety, and you are ready to experience real joy. It is good news because it gives hope. There is a solution! Emotional health is possible! There is a reliable source of joy, peace, and patience. Many have discovered it, and you can too.

VINE DRESSING

1. Can you think of any emotional health characteristic you desire that is not covered in the nine fruits of the Spirit (love, joy, peace, patience, kindness, goodness, faithfulness, gentleness, and self-control)?

    None

2. What would it be worth to you if you could get the fruit of the Spirit in pill form? What would you pay for a pill that brought lasting joy? What about a pill that brought perfect peace?

3. How does it make you feel to learn that the only source for the nine fruits of the Spirit is the Lord?

CHAPTER 4

GETTING
CONNECTED

In the previous chapters we learned that emotional health means possessing the fruit of the Spirit, and the source of the fruit of the Spirit is the Lord. So, here is the big question: How do we go about getting this fruit into our lives? It does no good to know the source if you do not also know the strategy to obtain it.

As a child, I toured the United States Mint in Washington and saw great stacks of money through thick security glass. I knew then the source of money, but what frustrated me was that I did not know how to get it. In this chapter, we are going to be very practical. My goal is to begin to show you how to *get the money*, so to speak! Since we now understand that stress, depression, and anxiety are symptoms of a deeper problem and that deeper problem is a lack of peace, joy, patience, and so on, we can learn the specific strategy that will set us free from those difficulties and replace them with the fruit of the Spirit.

Nourishment for Fruit Bearing

For fruit to grow and mature, it has to receive the nutrients that come from the ground. This is common sense. You cannot go to an apple orchard, cut off the limb of an apple tree, bring it home, set it in a window sill, and watch it grow beautiful apples. The limb will bear apples only if it is connected to the tree so that it can draw nourishment from the soil.

If you and I are going to grow the fruit of the Spirit, then we must also be connected to the tree or the vine so that we can receive nourishment. Without nourishment, the fruit will never mature in our lives. Without nourishment, we will not experience full-grown joy. Without nourishment, we will not experience mature peace. Without nourishment, we will experience none of the fruit of the Spirit in its sweet and ripened form.

So where does this nourishment come from? The nourishment comes from the Lord. This is why it is called the fruit *of* the Spirit. If I am going to bear the fruit of the Spirit in my life, then I must somehow be connected to the Lord (the Spirit) and receive nourishment from him. This is exactly what Jesus teaches us in the Gospel of John.

Let us look at two verses from John 15 where Jesus is giving instructions on how to have a close relationship with the Lord and the benefits that come from that kind of relationship.

Here is the first verse...

> I am the vine; you are the branches. If you remain in me
> and I in you, you will bear much fruit; apart from me
> you can do nothing.
>
> John 15:5 NIV

Here we see Jesus using an analogy similar to the fruit of the Spirit analogy. Jesus says that he, the Lord, is the vine. We are the branches. He states the obvious: If the branches are to bear fruit, they must be connected to the vine.

Let us not move on too quickly from this simple truth. There are few things in the Bible more important than this. The Lord wants to do many good things in our lives, and he underscores this in the first seventeen verses of John 15. However, the Lord will do none of this if we are not connected to him. Why is this? It is because what God does for us, God actually does through us, and the "through us" part requires a connection.

He shall be like a tree planted by the rivers of water, that brings forth its fruit in its season, whose leaf also shall not wither; and whatever he does shall prosper.
—PSALM 1:3

This truth is especially important when you focus on emotional health. How often do people pray that God will give them peace in life by changing their circumstances and taking away the things that bring stress? Of course there is nothing wrong with praying like this. (Certainly the Lord can do whatever he chooses to do.) However, this kind of prayer often betrays the fact that most of us do not understand how the Lord desires to work in our lives.

The Lord wants you to have peace, but not necessarily by him doing something for you. The Lord wants you to have peace by his doing something through you. In addition, the Lord cannot do something through you if you are not connected to him. Peace is not something that happens to you because your circumstances change. Peace is a fruit that grows in you because you are connected to the vine.

The same can be said of depression. As we have seen, depression is the result of a lack of joy. So how does a person gain joy? Does it come from a change in one's circumstances, different job, mended relationships, or more money? No, not the mature kind of joy that can withstand all of life's troubles. Lasting joy is not something that happens to you; it is something that grows in you because you are connected to the vine, which is the Lord.

Therefore, the first thing we learn from John 15:5 is that a connection to the Lord is essential to bear any of the fruit of the Spirit. Look at the last seven words of the verse.

"...apart from me you can do nothing."

Here Jesus says the same thing he does in the first part of the verse, but he states it as a negative. By doing so, he emphasizes the point: If you are not connected to the Lord, there is no hope of lasting fruit.

Let us look at another verse from John 15.

> Remain in me, and I will remain in you. No branch can
> bear fruit by itself; it must remain in the vine. Neither
> can you bear fruit unless you remain in me.
>
> John 15:4 NIV

Here we see the same warning we saw in the previous verse. Jesus tells us no branch can bear fruit by itself. In this verse he also says, "Neither can you bear fruit unless you remain in me."

Artificial Fruit

There is no way to have joy, peace, patience, kindness and gentleness apart from being connected to the vine. Some might ask, "Is there not some way we can artificially produce this fruit of the Spirit? Is there some other way to create this fruit in our lives?" The truth is: No. There is not. Any manufactured fruit is going to be temporary, unsatisfying, and vastly inferior to what the Lord promises to grow in us. Sometimes, I think that is the problem. We look for real fruit and then settle for artificial fruit.

Have you ever seen somebody set some artificial grapes, maybe some plastic oranges and apples, in a tray on a table? Those things can look very real. They can look delicious, sweet and satisfying. However, if you pick one up and try to take a bite out of it, I promise you, it will be completely unsatisfying. Moreover, the fruit we might manufacture by trying to improve our circumstances, or by trying to have a really good attitude, or by some kind of medication will be just as unsatisfying, in the long term, as the plastic grapes.

We look for real fruit, but we often settle for artificial fruit.

Recently I was counseling with a woman who shared that she was suffering from severe depression. I asked her what she did to treat her depression; what she did that sometimes made it better. She said the only thing she had found that would help her overcome her depression was shopping. Therefore, she would go shopping. She would get depressed, and then go spend money she really did not have to purchase things she really did not need. Then she would feel better.

I asked her how long the feeling of joy would last. How long was she free from depression? Did it help her overcome depression for six months or one month or even a week? She said, no. She said it made her feel good that day, but the next day she felt just as bad, if not worse. She felt worse because her depression had returned and now, on top of the depression, she had increased her money problems. (And this woman has completely devastated her family's finances.) All of this is because she is trying to produce artificial fruit.

I have seen people try to produce artificial fruits by shopping, with drugs (both legal and illegal), and with all sorts of destructive behavior. The truth is, none of that fruit is real. It will not be lasting, and it will not ultimately be satisfying. The only real fruit comes from being connected to the vine.

If you have ever had a glass of *Tang* (an orange-flavored drink made from powder and water) and a glass of freshly squeezed orange juice on the same day, then you know the difference between manufactured fruit and vine-grown fruit. You cannot improve on real fruit. You cannot improve on the fruit of the Spirit.

Therefore, we have seen the necessity of being connected to the Lord if we are going to experience any real, lasting emo-

Tang is a fruit-flavored breakfast drink. Originally formulated by General Foods Corporation food scientist William Mitchell, it was first marked in powdered form in 1959. Tang was famously used by some early NASA manned space flights.

—WIKIPEDIA

tional health. Next, I want us to learn the two critical parts involved in that connection. We will see the first one in this chapter and focus on the second one in the remainder of the book. Both parts are essential.

How To Get Connected

The Bible word for getting connected to the vine is salvation. A saved person is, by definition, connected to the Lord; an unsaved person is, by definition, not connected to the Lord. Therefore, salvation is the first step.

It is important to note that salvation is not the only step; it is simply the first step. Can a person be saved and still not have the fruit of the Spirit in his or her life? Absolutely. In fact, many people who are saved know nothing about the fruit of the Spirit and have very little evidence of the fruit in their lives. Salvation is not an automatic cure for depression or stress or anxiety or any other emotional difficulty. Nevertheless, salvation is the requisite first step if one has any hope of bearing the fruit of the Spirit in his or her life.

Can a person be saved and still not have the fruit of the Spirit in his or her life? Absolutely!

Some of you who are reading this book are in fact connected to the Lord through salvation. You have already taken that essential step. However, many people reading this book either have not yet taken the step or are unsure if they have taken the step. Whichever group you fall into, please do not skip this part of the book. Nothing else in this book will be of any value to you at all unless you have first nailed down this important connection.

The very good news is: You can connect to the Lord! You can have salvation today. I often speak with people, especially those struggling with depression, who believe that because of the circumstances of their lives or because of choices they've made in the past, they are no longer eligible to connect to the Lord. The Bible teaches that this kind of thinking is categorically untrue. There is no sin, and there is no circumstance that disqualifies you from salvation.

So, should you be saved today in order to trade your depression in for joy and your stress for peace? Well, no. While salvation does bring many benefits to our lives, not the least of which is the opportunity to bear the fruit of the Spirit. Salvation is not first about what we get from the Lord. Salvation is about recognizing who God is, who we are, what God has done for us, and what our response should be to him. Salvation is about believing in God, trusting God, loving God, and having a deep appreciation for what he has already done for us. Please do not view salvation as a self-improvement scheme or simply as a beat-depression-strategy. If you do, your faith will never be genuine and your relationship with God will never be real. Salvation is not a gimmick; salvation is a relationship.

Salvation is not first about what we get from the Lord.

How does salvation work?

The Bible teaches us that God is holy, pure, and righteous. The Bible also teaches us, even though it should really be apparent, that we are not holy, pure, or righteous. Every single reader of this book, just like the author, is guilty of sin. Every one of us is guilty of making wrong choices.

Our sin separates us from God. Because of our sin, none of us are connected to the vine.

Does this sound like bad news? It is, and it gets worse. Not only are we all sinners and guilty of sin, but we will all continue to be sinners. There is no self-improvement project that can change the fact that we are sinners. Even if you are successful at never sinning, never making any wrong or selfish choices ever again for as long as you live (as unlikely as that is), you would still be a sinner because of the choices you have made in the past.

Sounds bad? It gets worse. The Lord teaches in the Bible that what we deserve because of our sin is eternal death (Romans 6:23). That may seem harsh to us because we see our sin from the perspective of sinners, and consequently, our sin does not look so bad. However, the Lord sees our sin from the perspective of his perfect holiness and he has rightly judged that our sin merits eternal death.

Now for some good news. God loves us and he wants to forgive us and have a relationship with us. Therefore, God made a way.

Because God is a God of perfect justice, he cannot simply ignore our sin. So, God sent Jesus to take the punishment for our sins. Because I have sinned, someone must be punished for my sin. Jesus through his death on the cross did just that. Moreover, Jesus did it not only for me but also for you. You can be forgiven and have your relationship with God restored because of what Jesus did for you on the cross. Your sins have been paid for. This is good news.

> *Let the whole earth sing to the LORD! Each day proclaim the good news that he saves.*
> —1 CH. 16:23 NLT

While Jesus has done this for every person who will ever live, the only people who actually connect with God are those who respond to him; those who choose to accept this gift of forgiveness.

How can a person respond to the Lord and his great offer of salvation, forgiveness, and connection?

There are three simple words to help us understand how to respond: believe, trust, and surrender.

1. Believe

First, a person must believe that God is who he says he is in the Bible. This includes at least four things:

- Jesus is the son of God and Jesus is God.
- Jesus came and lived a sinless life on earth.
- Jesus died on the cross.
- Jesus rose from the grave.

2. Trust

A person must trust what Jesus has done for him or her on the cross as the only hope for the forgiveness of sins.

If I were to die today and stand before God and he were to ask me, "Why should I let you into my heaven?" What could I say? It would not be satisfactory for me to say I have been a good person or for me to point to some good deeds I have done in life. Why? Because while that might be true from my point of view, it is also true that I have sinned and because of my sin, I deserve death. I will never *deserve* to be connected with God based on my actions or my way-of-life. Now if God were to ask me that question, the only right response would be that I do not deserve to go to heaven, but I trust what Jesus has done on my behalf when he died on the cross.

3. Surrender

If I believe God is who he says he is, and I trust that he has done what he says he has done through Christ, then I must surrender my will to him. Surrender means I choose to allow him to be the Lord and master of my life. I allow him to change my heart, my mind, and my actions.

One of the words often used with surrender is repent. Repent means we make a change (or really we allow the Lord to make a change in us). We change from the sinful choices we made before we received salvation, and we change to making choices that please the Lord.

It is important here to note that while this change can often be dramatic; there is also a maturing process that must take place. None of us perfectly follows the Lord, but as we mature in our relationship with him, more and more changes become apparent. And the more we mature in our relationship with him, the more we see the Lord making the changes in us and through us.

> *Seek the LORD while you can find him. Call on him now while he is near.*
> —ISAIAH 55:6

Is this something you have done before? Has there ever been a time in your life when you understood your need for salvation? Has there ever been a time in your life when you understood how God, through Jesus, had provided for your salvation? Has there ever been a time in your life when you have expressed your belief, your trust, and your surrender to the Lord?

If you desire to do that right now, you can. You can simply pray and express your heart of trust and surrender to the Lord. Do not worry about using the right words. God's focus is on your heart and mind.

If you just did that then now you are a child of God and you are connected to the Lord.

> If you confess with your mouth that Jesus is Lord and believe in your heart that God raised him from the dead, you will be saved.
>
> Romans 10:9

Salvation is the first step in having the kind of connection with the vine that brings the nourishment to grow the fruit of the Spirit. In the next chapter, we will begin to learn the second step.

VINE DRESSING

1. What is the difference between the Lord doing something for you and the Lord doing something through you? Which does the Lord desire most to do?

   The Lord doing something through me shows a greater Glory to God, Helps me to be filled w/ the fruit of the Spirit.

2. What is the key to the Lord working through you? How is this similar to a vine producing grapes or an apple tree producing apples?

   Get Connected

3. Are you a child or God? Has there been a time in your life when you have called on the Lord to forgive you and save you? *I am a child of God*
   yes I have asked the Lord to forgive me

4. How can a person have a relationship with the Holy God? *Salvation*

5. Should a person call on the Lord for salvation simply as a means to find victory over depress and anxiety? What is the purpose of our salvation?

   it is the 1st Step

CHAPTER 5

GROWING THE FRUIT

Once a person is connected to the Lord, is depression automatically replaced with joy? Once a person is connected to the vine, is stress automatically replaced with peace? Do all Christians possess and showcase the fruit of the Spirit in their lives?

The answer is, emphatically, no.

Clearly many Christians suffer from emotional struggles the very same way those who are not connected to Christ struggle. Why is this? The key missing ingredient is something called *abiding*.

There is more to being a fruit-bearing Christian than simply getting connected to the vine. If a Christian is going to enjoy the mature fruit of the Spirit, then he or she must learn to abide in the vine. Few Christians know this basic truth. Fewer still do it.

This lack of abiding is why so many Christians struggle with depression, stress, and other emotional problems. This is why Christianity is sometimes criticized as not making a real difference in people's lives. Often people take the first step, they get connected. However, they fail to take the second step, the essential second step, which is abiding in the vine.

What is Abiding?

Let us go back to the teachings of Jesus we were reading in John 15, and do some Bible study. This will be easy to do, and it will be life changing.

> Abide in me, and I in you. As the branch cannot bear
> fruit by itself, unless it abides in the vine, neither can
> you, unless you abide in me.
>
> John 15:4

Notice the very first word in the verse: Abide. We see that word three times in this one verse. Moreover, we will see it again five more times in the next six verses. The word abide is one of the two or three most important words in the entire Bible.

What does it mean to abide in the Lord? *It means to be connected and to stay connected.* If we are abiding, then we are remaining over a period of time.

The best picture of the definition of abiding is the one Jesus uses here in John 15, but before we investigate this picture more closely, let us see a contemporary snapshot of abiding. My wife, daughters, and I love to have people over to our home. Almost every week we invite someone, and sometimes a bunch of someones, to come over for lunch or dinner. When people come over, we tell them to "make themselves at home," but we really don't mean it. As much as we enjoy their company and appreciate them honoring us by accepting our invitation, we eventually want them to go back to their own homes. They are temporary visitors. Cherished and valued visitors, but visitors nonetheless. On the other hand, there are four of us (and soon to be five, as we are in the process of bringing another daughter to

He who dwells in the shelter of the Most High will abide in the shadow of the Almighty.
—PSALM 91:1

our home through adoption) who live here. We are not just visitors. When the dinner party is over, we stay. Our stuff is here. Our hearts are here. Our home is here. We abide here!

That is what it means to abide, to connect and remain.

In fact, our pending adoption is a good picture of what should happen when we connect and abide with the Lord. When our new daughter arrives in our home for the first time, she will be different from all of the others who have visited our home. She will arrive, *think connect,* and then she will stay, *think abide.* This same kind of thing needs to happen in our relationship with the Lord.

Synonyms

Think through this list of synonyms for abide. Wrapping your head around this concept is key to bearing spiritual fruit.

- Remain
- Persist
- Linger
- Stick around
- Tarry
- Cleave
- Dwell
- Reside

Do you have a pretty good grasp on this key concept of abiding?

The Branch and The Vine

Jesus uses the image of grape vines and grapes. Think about how grapes grow on a vine. They do not grow instantly. It takes some time. In fact, sometimes it can take two or three years for good grapes to grow on a newly planted vine. Therefore, branches being connected to the vine for a moment or two is not sufficient to grow any fruit. No. The branches need time to soak up the rich sap produced in the roots and the vine. The fruit needs nutrients in order to grow and mature, and those nutrients come from the vine. If the branch is going to produce mature fruit, it must remain connected in a healthy way to the vine over a period of time. That is abiding.

Another word that helps us to understand the meaning of abide is the word sojourn. When I think of the word sojourn, I have a mental image of taking a long journey with someone. When we abide in Christ, we are taking a long journey. We are walking closely with him through life and eternity.

In another place in the Bible, we see two men walking with Jesus. The two men were going to stop for the night when it got late, and Jesus was going to go on. The two men encouraged Jesus to stop with them by saying "abide with us for it is toward evening and the day is far spent" (Luke 24:29, NKJ). Here we see the word abide used to mean to linger with or to stay with over a period of time.

Now focus again on the first few words of John 15:4. Jesus says, "Abide in me, and I in you." We see from this that abiding is a two-way relationship. It is a two-way relationship like most of our relationships are two-way. There is the part we do toward the Lord, and there is the part the Lord does toward us. This two-way nature will be important to remember when we begin to learn exactly how we abide in him in the next chapter.

In the second half of the verse, Jesus explains, as we have already noted in the previous chapter, that this abiding connection is the key to you and me bearing any spiritual fruit. He repeats this truth three times in three verses. But that is not all he says. Read the next verse:

> I am the vine; you are the branches. Whoever abides in me and I in him, he it is that bears much fruit, for apart from me you can do nothing.
>
> John 15:5

Here we see a restatement of the truth we learned in verse four. We also see an encouraging reference to how much fruit we can bear when we abide in him. Jesus says, "Whoever abides in me and I in him, he it is that bears much fruit!" How much of the fruit of joy can God bring to your life? How much of the fruit of peace, patience, kindness, goodness, gentleness and self-control can he bring to your life? Answer: Much fruit.

The fruit of the Spirit through abiding in Christ is not merely a subtle boost to your mood. It is a dramatic change of your entire disposition and constitution.

> If anyone does not abide in me he is thrown away like a branch and withers; and the branches are gathered, thrown into the fire, and burned.
>
> John 15:6

What happens to a branch that does not remain connected to the vine? It withers and dies, and it of course bears no fruit. What an accurate picture this is of so many people I speak with who are fighting their emotional difficulties with every strategy except abiding in Christ.

Key Elements in Abiding

> If you abide in me, and my words abide in you, ask whatever you wish, and it will be done for you.
>
> John 15:7

In this verse, we see the two key elements to abiding in Christ. *First, we see that when we abide in Christ, his words abide in us.* This means his words make their home in us. We cannot separate our experience of Jesus from our experience with his words. From our perspective in history, when we speak of the words of Jesus, we are talking about the Bible as a whole. In the next chapter, as we learn precisely how to abide in Christ, we will be talking a great deal about getting into his words and getting his words into us.

The second part of abiding we see in this verse is prayer, specifically answered prayer. Again, this is the focus of later chapters, but we learn here that these two things, God's word and prayer, are vitally connected.

> By this my Father is glorified, that you bear much fruit
> and so prove to be my disciples.
>
> John 15:8

Why does the Lord want us to bear spiritual fruit? Not only is it a blessing to us, and a blessing to those around us, it also brings glory and honor to the Lord. The world often sees people who claim to be disciples of Christ, but who also have a gloomy disposition, are tied in knots with stress and anxiety, and are living out-of-control lives. When this happens, it unfairly causes people to think less of the God we Christians claim to follow. However, when we live lives filled with the fruit of the Spirit, those around us cannot help but notice, and ultimately they will rightly attribute our character to our Lord. God will be praised and glorified.

> As the Father has loved me, so have I loved you. Abide
> in my love.
>
> John 15:9

The phrase at the end of verse nine is significant. Jesus says, "Abide in my love." That phrase speaks to the relationship that exists between the Lord and us when we are connected to and are abiding in him. Why does Christ desire so much to grow this fruit in our lives? It is because he loves us. As we abide in him and enjoy the fruit in our lives, we are enjoying the reward of his love.

He talks more about love in the next verse.

> If you keep my commandments, you will abide in my
> love, just as I have kept my Father's commandments
> and abide in his love.
>
> John 15:10

The word abide in this verse is connected to knowing and keeping the commandments of the Lord. Abiding in Christ is not just some warm fuzzy feeling or mere fondness for the Lord. It is real. It involves us making some choices and carrying out some commitments that will show up in life as obedience. We will learn more about this in the next chapter.

Source of Joy

> These things I have spoken to you, that my joy may be
> in you, and that your joy may be full.
>
> John 15:11

What a great verse! If we were not sure what Jesus was referring to when he talked about the kind of fruit we would bear, it is all cleared up here. He is talking about joy. Joy is the word used here to describe the entire basket of the fruit of the Spirit, and what an excellent word it is.

His Joy

Additionally, Jesus tells us three things about this joy. *First, he says it is "My joy."* The joy the Lord brings into your life through abiding is not the temporary, fleeting joy of the world. It is much more than that. It is the kind of joy that is experienced with the Father in eternity. In fact, the only other place in the New Testament where the Lord's joy is spoken of, it is said to be the reward given in heaven to the faithful servants of God (Matthew 25:21, 23). We learn from John 15:11, that when we abide in Christ and bear the fruit of the Spirit, we can experience a little bit of heaven here on earth.

Joy that Remains

The second thing we learn about this joy in this verse is that it is the joy that remains. For too many people, the story of their life is a rollercoaster of emotional difficulties. The fruit of the Spirit can smooth that out, at least to a degree. Joy from consistent abiding is consistent, remaining joy.

Full Joy

In addition, the third feature we learn about this joy is that it is full. What does "that your joy may be full" mean? With your mind's eye, picture a cup that is full of water. What do we mean when we say the cup is full? We mean that it cannot hold any more water. It has all the water it can hold. What do you mean when you tell someone at the end of a nice meal, that you are full? You mean you do not need any more food. You are satisfied.

Well, the Lord says, our joy will be full! The Lord will give us all of the joy we want and all of the joy we need. The Lord wants us to have such joy that we are satisfied. That is encouraging news!

Are you eager to know now how to abide in him?

VINE DRESSING

1. When a person is saved, does that mean they will never struggle with mental or emotional problems?

2. What is your best definition of abiding?

3. In Jesus' analogy, who is the vine? Who are the branches?

4. What is the responsibility of the vine?

5. What is the responsibility of the branches?

6. What happens if a branch does not stay connected to the vine?

7. How would your life be different if your joy was full (John 15:11)?

CHAPTER 6

APPOINTMENT FOR ABIDING

A biding involves many things, and learning how to abide in Christ will be a lifelong pursuit. One day, you will be much better at it than you are today, and the benefits you will enjoy from abiding will also be much greater. However, everyone must start somewhere. Where is that starting place?

Abiding begins with a daily appointment with the Lord. There should be a time every day that you spend listening and talking to the Lord. This is the first key to receiving regular nourishment from the vine. Practically speaking, there is no way to abide with the Lord if there is not a regular daily time when you focus on exactly that.

Think again of the analogy of the vine that Jesus used. For a branch to bear fruit it cannot occasionally attach to the vine, it must continually attach to the vine. The branch does not have within itself the resources needed to produce fruit. You and I do not have within ourselves the resources needed to produce spiritual fruit. In order to have real lasting fruit the branch must continually connect to the vine. You and I must continually connect to the Lord. The best first step to that happening is to have a daily appointment with the Lord.

God desires to do something through you, but God cannot work through you on a daily basis if he is not connected to you on a daily basis.

Another way to see the importance of this daily appointment is to look at this from the point of view of a relationship. How do two people gain a stronger personal relationship? The easy answer is that they spend time together. It does not matter how much you have in common with someone or how much you love him or her, if you only spend a total of one hour per year together, you will never have a close relationship. If you desire for that relationship to be closer and more meaningful then you must choose to spend more time with that person.

If you and I desire to have a closer and more meaningful relationship with the Lord then we must spend time with him daily. If we desire to have the kind of relationship with the Lord that makes a difference in our emotional health then we must make it a priority to meet with him daily.

Remember God desires to do something through you, but God cannot work through you on a daily basis if he is not connected to you on a daily basis.

Something Old or Something New?

When I speak of spending time daily with the Lord, it may sound like I am referring to something Christians often call a devotional time or a quiet time. It is true I am speaking of something like that, but not exactly like that. What many Christians call a devotional time or quiet time is not helpful in our desire to abide in the Lord. For many Christians, when it comes to having a daily quiet time, their intentions are good, but sadly, their practice is ineffective.

It is unlikely you have ever had a devotional time like I am going to describe!

I want to show you a way to spend time with God daily. This is a method that you can actually do. This is a method that you will enjoy. This is a method through which you will gain nourishment, and because of that, you will bear spiritual fruit. In fact, to help remind us that this is something different, we will call it "an appointment with God" instead of calling it a devotional time or a quiet time.

Traditional Devotions

First, let me describe the traditional way of having a devotional time, and show you why this is ineffective.

For many Christians their devotional time is simply a task they believe they should try to mark off their list each day. Many Christians use a devotional book that gives them a paragraph or two or a brief story written by the author, and one or two verses of Scripture. They read through that quickly, and then they pray. The prayer is usually brief. Often the prayer is simply the recitation of a previously prepared list. Whether it is from a list or not, it usually sounds much like the prayer they prayed the previous day. Moreover, it seldom has anything to do with what they just read.

Here are the likely results of approaching devotional time like that:

- Sometimes people feel like they have accomplished something because they have marked it off their list or because they have been consistent for a certain number of days. God must be pleased with them because they have done their morning duty. *Never mind that they cannot tell you one life change that has resulted from those few minutes they spent in their devotional time today, yesterday, or any day.*

- Sometimes people feel guilty because they missed their devotional time because they were busy with other things.

- Sometimes people feel guilty because they are concerned they may not have spent sufficient minutes or read enough verses in their devotional time.

None of those results has anything to do with abiding in Christ. That approach may bring temporary satisfaction or it may bring guilt, but it has nothing to do with building a relationship. Let me give you a new way of having a devotional time or quiet time that I believe can change your life.

A New Kind of Devotions

Think of your devotional time as a time of building a relationship, not completing a task. You are not simply trying to mark something off your list. You are trying to get to know the Lord.

Imagine having a relationship with a friend where you feel like you have to call him or her x number of times a week and spend x number of minutes each time talking to him or her. So, one day you call him up, apologize that you did not call the previous day, and apologize that you are fourteen minutes behind your allotted relationship schedule thus far this month.

Think of your devotional time as a time of building a relationship, not completing a task.

That would be absurd. If you really want to have a closer relationship with your friend, then you will spend as much time as possible with him. You will not count the number of times or the number of minutes. You will simply devote yourself to the relationship. That is how we should think of this appointment with the Lord.

I remember when my wife and I were dating prior to being married. For about three months, she lived ten states away due to her job. We talked on the phone every night. I did not count the minutes. I did not measure our conversations. I missed her so much. I could not wait to call her each night and spend time together on the phone. Then the phone bill arrived. I was shocked at how much we had talked and how much it had cost. That is the nature of a relationship. Our conversations were driven by a desire to be close, not an obligation to mark off a task completed.

Another way to look at this is to think of this appointment with the Lord as eating a meal as opposed to taking a pill. It is a strange comparison, but read on. I take a vitamin each morning not because I enjoy vitamins or because I look forward to taking one each day, but simply because somebody told me it would make me healthier. I am not exactly sure how or why it will make me healthier, and I am not completely convinced it will. However, I do it each day because for some reason I just think it is what people ought to do.

Think of this appointment with the Lord as eating a meal as opposed to taking a pill.

That routine is exactly how the average Christian approaches his or her devotional time. This is not good. Think about how different your approach is to eating a meal than taking a pill. Think of how you look forward to eating a fabulous meal with someone you love and enjoy spending time. You do not count the number of minutes you are sitting at the table. You do not ask what is the least amount of food you can eat and it still count as a meal. You just enjoy it. This is how we should approach our appointment with the Lord.

Therefore, here are three questions you should *never* ask yourself during your devotional time:

- How many minutes am I spending?
- How many verses am I reading?
- How much am I writing down?

Moreover, here are the questions you should *always* ask yourself during your devotional time:

- Am I growing closer to the Lord?
- Is the Lord pleased with our time together?
- How is my appointment with God impacting the rest of my day?

Getting Started

What do I need to do to get started with this new approach to devotional time?

Remember, this is the most crucial step if you are going to experience joy instead of depression, peace instead of stress, and patience instead of anxiety! So, do not skip this.

First, you need to find a room where you can be alone. It is important to have a place where you will not be distracted. Jesus often withdrew from distractions to spend time with the Father.

> After he had dismissed the crowds, he went up on the mountain by himself to pray. When evening came, he was there alone.
>
> Matthew 14:23

> Jesus would withdraw to desolate places and pray.
>
> Luke 5:16

You need a place where you do not feel like somebody is watching you or critiquing you. Maybe for you this is the dining room before anyone else in the house wakes up in the morning. Maybe for you it is an office or computer room where you can go and shut the door. Maybe for you it is the bedroom, but I do not advise you doing this in bed. You will see why in a moment.

Next, you need a Bible you can read easily. It should be an actual Bible translation and not a paraphrase of the Bible. If you do not know which you have, look for the word *translation* on the title page. The most common ones are the

New International Version (NIV), the New King James Version (NKJ), and the English Standard Version (ESV). All of those are good. The Bible I recommend most often for people beginning these kinds of devotional times is the New Living Translation (NLT). The NLT may not be the very best study Bible, but it is a great devotional Bible. By the way, having a study Bible with added notes and commentary is not a necessity, although sometimes it is helpful. One more note: I suggest you do not do your Bible reading on your computer. There are too many distractions with emails and the internet. Let this be a distraction free, personal time with your Lord.

You also need a notebook and a pen. It is important that you are able to write things down. This is why you should not do this in bed. You need to be in a place where you can easily and comfortably write things down.

It is also important to *have a designated time to have your appointment with the Lord.* The very best time, the time that will benefit you the most, is first thing in the morning. Jesus is seen in the gospels praying early in the morning:

> Rising very early in the morning, while it was still dark, Jesus departed and went out to a desolate place, and there he prayed.
>
> Mark 1:35

Another time of the day will work, as long as the time is consistent, but nothing is as valuable as starting off your day in communication with the Lord.

There is a certain perspective or view you should have as you approach your appointment with the Lord. You should **view the Bible as the Lord's personal letter to you.** You are not reading it as a history book or a theology textbook. In your devotional time, you should view all of your reading with the true thought that the Lord has written this for you, for now. Imagine that the Lord is present with you while you read. (By the way, he is.) Imagine that you can talk with the Lord as you read and he can answer

> *You should view the Bible as the Lord's personal letter to you.*

you through his word and by speaking to your spirit. (By the way, you can, and he can, and he will.)

Steps for the Daily Appointment

1. Focus on the Lord

Once you are alone and you have your Bible, a notebook and a pen, then it is time to begin. The first thing you want to do is get your focus upon the Lord. The best way to do this is to begin with prayer. The reason why prayer is important is it helps get our mind off the regular distractions of life and get it focused on the Lord. If I am especially distracted such that I am having a hard time focusing, I begin by quoting or reading the Lord's Prayer aloud.

> Our Father in heaven, may your name be kept holy. May your Kingdom come soon. May your will be done on earth, as it is in heaven. Give us today the food we need, and forgive us our sins, as we have forgiven those who sin against us. And don't let us yield to temptation, but rescue us from the evil one.
>
> Matthew 6:9-13 NLT

I do not quote it in a hurried fashion. I say it slowly, focusing on its meaning. I say it as if I were talking directly to the Lord, because I am. While I do not always say or quote the Lord's prayer, ordinarily when I do, it really helps me begin to concentrate upon the Lord.

Following that, I continue to pray for a few minutes using a little bit of a formula to get things started but also praying in a little more of a personal way. Before the appointment is over I am going to pray in a very personal manner, but in the beginning, I follow this formula: C.H.A.T. I have a brief chat with the Lord.

C. H. A. T.
Confess
Honor
Ask
Thank

The letter C stands for confess. I spend time confessing any sin that is in my life. To confess sin, I tell God everything I have done that is wrong that I have not previously confessed. I then agree with him that those actions or attitudes are sin. I ask for his forgiveness and for his help to make a change with respect to that sin in the future. Sometimes at this point I just sit quietly and wait for the Lord to remind me of failures or bad attitudes I have had the previous day. Often there will be sins I have been too calloused to notice.

If we confess our sins, he is faithful and just to forgive us our sins and to cleanse us from all unrighteousness.
—1 JOHN 1:9

Without fail, the Lord brings those things to mind. When he does, I confess them.

The letter H stands for honor. I spend some time honoring the Lord for who he is. I spend just a few moments focusing on his Holiness or on his goodness or on his mercy or on his power. On some days, I struggle with exactly what to say in this part of my prayer. When I struggle in this section, I usually try to quote the words from one of the praise songs we sang in our church worship service the previous week.

The letter A stands for ask. Here I spend a few moments asking the Lord to give me a quality time with him this morning. I ask him to help me focus on him and his word. I ask him to speak to me through his word and help me to be faithful to the things I read today.

The letter T stands for thanks. I spend a few moments expressing to the Lord how thankful I am for the good things he has done for me. I usually thank him for my salvation. I thank him for my family. I thank him for all of the things that rise to the forefront of my mind at this time.

When I come to the end of my prayer of thanksgiving in my chat with the Lord, without fail, my focus is entirely upon him.

2. Abide in God's Word

The second part of my appointment with God is abiding in God's Word. This is where I read the Bible and listen for what God has to say to me today.

In the beginning, I suggest that you do this reading from the New Testament or the book of Proverbs. You can have a great appointment with the Lord while reading in the Old Testament but it may be more difficult and require a little more experience at having these regular devotional times. Take a few laps through the New Testament and the book of Proverbs before you dive into the Old Testament. Start in the New Testament wherever you would like; maybe start in the book of James, or perhaps the gospel of John. Once you start reading a book in the New Testament, continue to read from that book each day until you have completed the book. This is much better than just skipping around each day. I would also suggest you keep a tally of where you have read so you know you have read the entire New Testament before you begin again.

The law of the LORD is perfect, converting the soul; The statutes of the LORD are right, rejoicing the heart; More to be desired are they than gold, yea, than much fine gold; sweeter also than honey and the honeycomb.

—Psalm 19:7-10

When you read, you should read to hear. With every verse of Scripture, you should be asking the Lord what he is trying to teach you today in that verse. Not every single verse will have a life application lesson. In fact, sometimes you may have to read many verses before you feel the Lord is showing you something for your own life. Sometimes it may seem like the Lord shows you something in every verse you read.

When you feel like the Lord is showing you something important for your life, then you should write it down. When we write things down they become fixed in our heart and mind. When we write something down, we show that we really believe it is important. If a friend called today and said you had won a $1 million prize, but in order to claim it you had to have a claim number, and then he told you the number, what would you do? You would write it down! Why? Because it is important. When something is important, we write it down.

What should you write down?

- If the Lord shows you something you should do...

- If the Lord shows you something you should be reminded of...

- If the Lord shows you a new way to look at things...

- If the Lord shows you a new attitude to strive for...

- If the Lord shows you a change you should make...

- If the Lord shows you something you should be more thankful for...

- If the Lord shows you or reminds you of a special reason you should praise him...

If it is important, you should write it down.

So, how many verses should you read? That is the wrong question. When you think about how many verses you should read, this appointment with the Lord can easily turn into a task that you are trying to mark off your to do list. Remember this is not marking off a task; this is about building a relationship. So how many verses should you read? *Read as many as you want to read!* Some days you may read a great number of verses; some days you may read only a paragraph or two. The point is not how much you read; the point is how much you hear from the Lord.

There have been times when I have read six verses and the Lord has shown me six to eight things I needed to know or to do. Once I had processed all of that, I was finished reading for the day. However, there have been days when I have read chapters and chapters. Just keep focusing on building the relationship instead of counting the verses, and you will not go wrong.

What about Bible reading plans like "through the Bible in a year" and others? Those are not bad things, and I have done those in the past, and I am currently doing one. The problem is, these plans can make your appointment with God more about reading a certain number of verses or chapters, and you can miss the whole hearing-from-the-Lord part of this. Remember that reading the Bible through in a year is not the same thing as abiding in the Lord.

All Scripture is breathed out by God and profitable for teaching, for reproof, for correction, and for training in righteousness, that the man of God may be complete, equipped for every good work.
—2 TIMOTHY 3:16-17

My suggestion is that while you are still learning to have this appointment with the Lord that you just read to hear. Some days you will read fifteen verses and not be able to write down all of the critical stuff the Lord is communicating to you. Some days, as I said earlier, you will read a number of chapters. If you want to do a Bible reading plan, perhaps that could be something separate from your appointment with the Lord. You could do your appointment with the Lord as you go through the New Testament in the morning and then do the big Bible reading plan just before you go to bed each night.

3. Have a Heart-to-Heart

The third part of your appointment with God is a time of very personal prayer.

The first things I pray for are those things the Lord has shown me in my Bible reading that day. Often times there are things I should do that come out of that. I pray about those things. I pray that God will give me wisdom to know how to do them. I pray that God will give me the commitment and the faithfulness I need to accomplish them. Often in my Bible reading, the Lord will point out to me sins or sinful attitudes that need to be confessed. I pray about those things. Therefore, the first part of my prayer is simply a review of what the Lord has shown me in my Bible reading. The notes I made while reading become an outline for the first part of my prayer time.

> *Listen to my voice in the morning, LORD. Each morning I bring my requests to you and wait expectantly.*
> —PSALM 5:3

The second part of my prayer is difficult to describe. Here I just bare my heart before the Lord. I pray for his help in the areas I most need him. I pray for his wisdom in the areas I am most in need of guidance. I pray for people I love. If I have fears, I pray about that. If I have doubts, I pray about that. If I am angry about something, I pray about that.

With each thing I pray for I make a little note in my notebook. I do not usually write out the prayer, and often times the note would make sense to nobody but me, but I always jot a few words with each item of prayer. It is easy to get distracted during your prayer time. I have found that jotting down a few brief notes as I pray helps keep me focused. One thing to note though: I do not jot down a list and then pray.

To me that would tend to make this feel like a task instead of a relationship. I just jot down some notes as I pray. I do not start with a prayer list; I finish with one.

Time To Start!

Having this daily appointment with the Lord is so important in abiding. It is so vital in building the relationship. It is key in replacing emotional struggles with spiritual health. Nothing you can do will bring more of the fruit of the Spirit (love, joy, peace, patience, etc.) faster and more effectively than having this daily appointment with the Lord.

You should make yourself a student of how to do this better. There are many great books devoted to this subject. Find them. Read them. (You can visit my website, *www.IlluminatingTheDarkness.com*, for a list of recommended books.) Talk with people who have been walking closely with the Lord for decades, and ask them to share about their devotional life with you. There is a learning curve. You will not be an expert at this overnight. Nevertheless, few things in life will pay greater dividends than investing your life in learning to do this better.

VINE DRESSING

1. Have you ever tried to have a regular quiet-time or devotional time before? How successful were you? What impact did it have in your daily life?

2. If you have had quiet-times or devotional times before, why do you think they were not more successful with helping you enjoy emotional health and strength?

3. In a relationship between two people who desire to be close, how important is it that they spend time together?

4. What are the three questions you should always be asking about your devotional times with the Lord?

5. What is the best place for you to have your daily appointment with the Lord? What is the best time of day for you?

6. What do you need to do or get to begin your new daily times with the Lord? Do you have a Bible you can easily read? Notebook and pen?

CHAPTER 7

THE POWER OF THE APPOINTMENT

J esus promises us if we abide in him and we abide in his word that we will bear much fruit. Isn't it exciting to know that if you are connected to the Lord and you develop a daily habit of having an appointment with God then you are on the path to emotional health and strength? Isn't it exciting to know that the buds will have formed in your life that will, if you continue to abide, soon produce the sweet fruits of the Spirit?

To be honest though, I need to deal with an objection you may have. I am sure someone will read this book to this point and think, "Okay, I had my appointment with the Lord yesterday and nothing happened. My depression, stress and anxiety have not improved one bit. What went wrong?"

Four words help us understand the science of how a daily appointment with God can bring such changes in our lives. Once we understand these words, we will not be discouraged. Instead, this new perspective will give us hope. The words are time, passion, consistency, and compounding.

Time

How long does it take fruit to grow and ripen on the vine? Obviously, it does not happen overnight. There is a reason why the Bible uses the analogy of fruit to refer to emotional health. The Bible could have used the anal-

The Bible intentionally uses the analogy of the fruit of the Spirit and not the gift or letter of the Spirit in part to emphasize the time that is required.

ogy of a gift, "the gift of the Spirit." The Bible could have used the analogy of a letter from the spirit. Both of those analogies would imply that emotional health comes immediately, like a gift or a letter. However, the Lord chose to use the analogy of fruit on the vine because he wanted us to understand the principle of staying connected to the vine, but just as important, he wanted us to understand that real emotional health and strength take time.

If your neighbor were to plant a garden on Monday, and then dig it up in frustration on Friday because he did not have any vegetables to pick, you would call him a fool. Let us not make the same mistake as we wait for the fruit of the Spirit to ripen and mature in our own lives.

This does not mean we should lower our expectations. As you will see when we get to the last of these four words, there is no reason to lower expectations. There is, in fact, probably a pretty good reason to raise expectations. So, let us have the right kind of understanding. Let us remember that the sweetest fruit is the fruit that has had time to mature on the vine.

Passion

The point of being connected to the Lord and abiding in the Lord is not primarily that we will feel better. Having emotional health is the byproduct of having a passion for the Lord expressed through abiding in him. The fruit of the Spirit is a fringe benefit of having a close relationship with the Lord.

Our focus should be on getting to know the Lord better and loving him more. When we do that, we will begin to see the fruit of the Spirit the Lord bears in our lives. Do not concentrate on the fruit; concentrate on the relationship.

Consistency

Consistency is the key to success in almost every area of life.

Let us think about how to be successful in exercise. Do you think one long hard day of exercising every six to eight weeks would have much benefit? No. The secret to gaining real benefits from exercise is in exercising consistently. Forty minutes a day, five days a week is much more beneficial than twelve hours one day of the month.

Let us think about taking vitamins. Which is better for maintaining good health, sitting down a couple times a year and taking 180 vitamins each time? Or would the benefit come from simply taking one small vitamin each day?

How about being a good father or a

Consistency is the key to success in almost every area of life.

good husband? Do you think my wife and girls would be okay with me neglecting them most of the year if for one week each year I was super dad and hero husband? No, my wife and girls want me to be caring and loving every single day.

When it comes to having your appointments with God the real benefit is going to come from doing this daily; doing this consistently.

Let me describe the typical Christian's walk with the Lord in a year.

- Fifty days of poor and ineffective quiet times...

- Six days of guilt induced quiet times...

- Eight days of emergency quiet times...

- One year of struggling with one or more of the big three emotional monsters called depression, stress and anxiety...

If we are actually going to bear spiritual fruit, we must be consistent with this daily appointment with God. If we are hit and miss with our daily appointment, or if we stop having our daily appointment, then the fruit of the Spirit will quickly disappear in our lives.

Think of how you put gasoline in your car. If all of a sudden you stop being consistent about filling your car with gasoline, your car will run out of gas, and it will stop. At that point, you can plead with your car all you want. You can show it gas receipts for all the years you gave it fuel regularly. You can remind it of all the times you have filled it all the way to the top. You can talk to it about the times you used premium gasoline. However, I am telling you, the car will not start.

The fruit of the Spirit is completely dependent upon you abiding consistently with the Lord.

Compounding

The last word refers to the benefits of having a daily appointment with the Lord, and this is a very exciting truth.

Here is the principle: The longer you do this, and the more consistently you do this, the more and more valuable it will be.

This means, if you are faithful and consistent to abide in the Lord for a few days your *attitude* will change. If you are faithful and consistent to abide in the Lord for a few weeks, your *character* will change. If you are faithful and consistent to abide in the Lord for a year, your *life* will change. For ten years, your *world* will change!

There is a compounding effect to the work we do in building a close relationship with the Lord. The longer you are consistent, the greater the payoff, and the payoff increases exponentially.

Let me illustrate the power of compounding by looking at its effect on saving money. If someone puts back five dollars per week beginning at birth and he is consistent to do that until he is 65 years old, assuming the average stock market return holds true for those 65 years, he would retire with $4.7 million. That is a lot of money, especially when you consider the investment was a meager five dollars per week. How can a total investment of less than $17,000 (five dollars per week) turn into $4.7 million? It is because of the power of compounding interest.

If you are consistent to abide in the Lord for a few days your attitude will change. If you are consistent to abide in the Lord for a few weeks, your character will change. If you are consistent to abide in the Lord for a year, your life will change. For ten years, your world will change!

I know people who have been consistently abiding in the Lord for so many years that when I read the description of the fruit of the Spirit, I immediately think of those people. Moreover, I do not believe any circumstance, any tragedy, or any disappointment could ever cause those people to lose their joy and peace. How can that be true? It is because of the compounding effect of consistently abiding in the Lord.

I have read stories of people who have been executed for their faith in the Lord yet have remained firm and steadfast and filled with the fruit of the Spirit until their very last breath. How can somebody have that kind of strength of character? It is because of the compounding effect of consistently abiding in the Lord.

What is the lesson we learn from these four words? The sooner you begin the process, the more you love the Lord, the more consistent you are with abiding, the greater the change the Lord will bring in your life.

VINE DRESSING

1. What is your expectation of how long it will take before you notice spiritual fruit growing in your life? Are you ready to be committed for that long?

2. What role does consistency play in bearing quality fruit?

3. Because of the compounding effect of this consistent time with the Lord, you could be a remarkably different person six months or a year from now. How does that make you feel?

CHAPTER 8

FOCUS IS THE
PARTNER OF ABIDING

A biding does not end or take a break when you get up from your appointment with the Lord. The appointment with the Lord, your devotional time, is an essential part of abiding, but it is not all of abiding. Think back to our analogy of the branch and the vine. It is important that the branches are continually connected to the vine so they can receive nourishment. The good news is there is a way to have that constant connection, and that is the next part of abiding.

We will call this part of abiding, *focusing* upon the Lord. As we go about our everyday tasks and we face our everyday struggles we should do so with a constant focus upon our relationship with the Lord.

Here is why that is important. Our focus determines both our emotional and even our biological response to our surroundings. It is easy to find examples of this. Take for instance the watching of a very sad movie. You focus on the somber movie for a couple of hours and what happens? You are saddened. Some people will even be brought to tears. This is a perfect example of how focus determines emotional and biological response.

Our focus determines both our emotional and even our biological response to our surroundings.

Another good example is how certain things make us angry. I imagine I could begin to write about some things and describe some things that would make you very angry. What would happen as you focused on my words? Your blood pressure would increase. Your face might turn red. You would be tempted to raise your voice or maybe beat on the table. There would be both an emotional and physical response because of your focus.

If we will focus on the Lord, especially when we face difficult or stressful times, the result will be that we will enjoy the fruit of the Spirit in our lives despite the difficulties. I am amazed at how God will give me a real sense of joy and peace when I get into stressful situations or when something happens that could easily depress or discourage me, and I choose to keep my focus upon him.

We see this principle, among other places, in Proverbs:

As a man thinks in his heart, so he is.

Proverbs 23:7 NKJ

This verse teaches us that whatever we focus on will determine our character and our emotional state. I have known people who fill their lives with what I call *stinking thinking*. They focus on how hard life is. They focus on how unfair people have treated them. They focus on all the obstacles that are before them. They focus on their failures and shortcomings. And that focus has filled their heart with anger, strife, depression, stress, and so on.

When I am counseling with these people, I try to encourage them to change their focus to the Lord. I plead with them to do this because I know a new focus will bring real changes in them. I have seen people's lives changed in less than a day because they changed their focus. Unfortunately, I have also seen people who either could not or would not change their focus and consequently their life never changed.

On a side note, do you know why some people are unable to change their focus and other people can change their focus easily? It depends largely on whether or not a person is having a daily, consistent appointment with the Lord. It is through that appointment that the Lord gives us the strength to change our focus to him. Without the daily time with the Lord, most people will find it very difficult to really change their focus for any significant period of time.

So how exactly do we abide through focusing on the Lord? There are three important steps.

Step 1: Prayer

The first thing we must do is pray. This is not the same kind of prayer you prayed in your appointment with the Lord. This is a constant and subtle conversation that you have with the Lord throughout the day. Look at the unusual command we are given in First Thessalonians:

Pray without ceasing.

1 Thessalonians 5:17

How can someone pray without ceasing? Well, it is a little bit like talking to yourself except your focus is upon the Lord and the Lord will respond. As I go through my day, I am constantly, in my mind, thanking the Lord for the little things that happen in my life that are good. I am constantly asking the Lord for wisdom and guidance as I make decisions and as I speak with people. I am constantly asking the Lord to bear spiritual fruit in my life as I face difficult circumstances. I am constantly asking that I might have joy instead of depression, peace instead of stress, patience instead of anxiety.

It is amazing what God can do through you as long as you stay connected to him throughout the day via this unusual style of prayer.

There are many Bible verses emphasizing the importance of focusing on the Lord in prayer. Let me give you one more.

Is anyone among you suffering? Let him pray. Is anyone cheerful? Let him sing praise.

James 5:13

What should we do when we suffer? We should pray. What should we do when we desire to be more cheerful? We should pray and praise. The reference to singing songs is talking about singing songs of praise to the Lord, which is simply prayer set to music.

So to keep our focus upon the Lord throughout the day we should pray throughout the day.

Step 2: Thinking

The second way we keep our focus upon the Lord through the day is by spending our time thinking about godly things. If I spend my day thinking about how unfair I think life is, or how poorly someone has treated me, then that *stinking thinking* will do nothing but rob me of spiritual fruit.

Certainly, difficult things will happen. People may mistreat me; I will have to deal with failures; there will be disappointment. Nevertheless, none of these things necessitate that I dwell on them. Listen to what the Bible says to do in Philippians 4:8:

> Whatever is true, whatever is honorable, whatever is just, whatever is pure, whatever is lovely, whatever is commendable, if there is any excellence, if there is anything worthy of praise, think about these things.
>
> Philippians 4:8

So what should I be thinking about as I have spare moments in the day? Maybe I will spend time thinking about what I learned in my Bible reading this morning. Maybe I will spend some time thinking about the good things God is doing in my life and the lives of people I know. Maybe I will open up my Bible and spend a few minutes reading when I have a break in the day. Maybe I will listen to some Christian music that encourages me as I work. Maybe I will spend time with other believers who practice focusing on the Lord through their days.

His delight is in the law of the LORD, and on his law he meditates day and night. He is like a tree planted by streams of water that yields its fruit in its season... In all that he does, he prospers.
—PSALM 1:2-3

The decisions we make about what we think on will determine whether or not the Lord is going to bear spiritual fruit in our lives when we most need it during the day.

Looking to the future

For some people this part will seem extreme, but it is biblical advice, and it works! When we go through difficult times, we should remind ourselves that the time we have in this life is short, and what really matters, for those people who are children of the Lord, is the life which is to come.

When my wife, my girls and I are on a long car trip, my girls usually complain about how frustrating it is to sit in the car hour after hour. When they do this, I try to remind them that the destination will be worth the journey. Is it worth spending 10 hours in the backseat of a car in order to be able to spend 10 days at the beach? Yes indeed!

There will be difficulties in this life. None of us should be surprised. Some of those difficulties may be extreme. What should we do? We should keep things in perspective. Ultimately, what matters is not our comfort and leisure in the very few years we spend in this life, but what ultimately matters is how we will spend eternity with the Lord.

Listen to the truth we read in 2 Corinthians 4:17:

> Our present troubles are quite small and won't last very long. Yet they produce for us an immeasurably great glory that will last forever!
>
> 2 Corinthians 4:17 NLT

In this verse, the writer reminds us that our current difficulties are quite small compared to the great inheritance awaiting us in heaven.

With that in mind, see the counsel the writer gives us in the very next verse...

> We don't look at the troubles we can see right now;
> rather, we look forward to what we have not yet seen.
> For the troubles we see will soon be over, but the joys
> to come will last forever.
>
> 2 Corinthians 4:18 NLT

So what are we to do? We are not to focus upon the present troubles any more than is necessary. We are to focus upon the joy that will last forever in heaven.

Have you ever wondered how Jesus was able to face the suffering he had to endure on the cross? How could he have so much courage knowing the extent of the pain of the nails and the separation he would experience from his heavenly Father? The Bible gives us the answer:

> We do this by keeping our eyes on Jesus, on whom our
> faith depends from start to finish. He was willing to
> die a shameful death on the cross because of the joy he
> knew would be his afterward. Now he is seated in the
> place of highest honor beside God's throne in heaven.
>
> Hebrews 12:2 NLT

This verse teaches us we are to keep our eyes, our focus, upon Jesus. It then shows us how he was able to endure the experience on the cross. He was able to endure because he kept his focus upon the joy that awaited him in the future and in heaven.

Can You Do This?

Yes, you can do this. I know it can sound overwhelming when you just begin to think about focusing upon the Lord all day long, but this is not just some positive thinking exercise. Remember abiding is a two-way relationship. As you focus upon the Lord, he will draw nearer to you. Once you commit yourself to this, it will be easier and better than you probably think.

In the book of James, we read this encouraging verse...

Draw near to God, and He will draw near to you.

James 4:8

The wisdom of this verse will be evident to you when you seek to focus upon the Lord. The more you focus on him the more he will draw near to you. There is some effort needed on your part to focus, but know that the Lord is going to honor that, and he will be drawing near to you too.

This Gets Easier!

You will discover two things as you focus upon the Lord. *The first thing is that this gets easier with experience.* Several years ago, my wife and I had a small monogramming business. Before we started the business, I knew absolutely nothing about monogramming. However, once I got into the business I learned about the different stitches and how some stitches need to go in one direction and some stitches need to go in a different direction in order for the monogrammed name or logo to look right. After that, every time I saw a monogrammed ball cap or handbag I immediately noticed how the stitching was done. Who knows how many thousands of monogrammed items I had seen in my life before that point and had never noticed even once the direction of the stitching.

He fulfills the desire of those who fear him; he also hears their cry and saves them.
—PSALM 145:19

However, once I began to learn more about the monogramming the more I noticed the stitching in items I would see every day.

I could not write enough chapters to explain to you the things you will begin to see and learn about the Lord and how he works day by day as you excel in focusing on him. This is something you have to experience for yourself. All I can tell you is that this gets easier with time.

God's Hand Gets Clearer!

The second thing you will discover is that the hand of God in your life will become clearer and more evident to you the longer you do this. If I were to ask you to close your eyes and then name all of the red things that are in the room you are in right now, you would probably be hard pressed to name very many. However, if I then asked you to open your eyes and scan the room for red things you would discover many. What is the lesson? You see the things you are looking for.

And when you begin to focus upon the Lord and look moment by moment for his hand in your life, then you will see things you have never seen before.

This leads us right into the last part of abiding and perhaps the part that can bring the biggest change in your life the quickest: thankfulness.

VINE DRESSING

1. What is the connection between what we focus on and our emotional state? What personal examples can you think of?

2. What does it mean to "pray without ceasing?"

3. What are some practical strategies to help you keep your focus on the Lord throughout the day?

4. How can a focus on Heaven, our eternal home, help us in daily living?

5. The Lord promises that if you draw near to him, he will draw near to you. How does that make you feel?

CHAPTER 9

THANKFULNESS
GOD'S WONDER DRUG

W hat if there were a wonder drug for the treatment of depression, stress, anxiety, and every other emotional ailment? Wouldn't it be wonderful if there were actually one thing a person could do, or eat, or read, or take that would eliminate or greatly diminish the effects of all his or her emotional struggles in life?

I believe there is just such a wonder drug. This drug cannot be purchased at the drugstore. A doctor cannot prescribe it. This wonder drug is, in fact, available to everyone. It will be most effective in the life of a person who is abiding in the Lord, but to be honest, this wonder drug will improve the emotional health of any person who tries it.

So what is this wonder drug? It is simple thankfulness.

I know that may not sound like a life-changing idea, but it can be, and it is. The truth is, your emotional health could be markedly better than it is right now in one short hour, if you would do the things I show you in this chapter. I have seen this truth completely transform people who give it a chance.

Look how the Bible describes this incredible truth...

> Do not be anxious about anything, but in everything by prayer and supplication with thanksgiving let your requests be made known to God. And the peace of God, which surpasses all understanding, will guard your hearts and your minds in Christ Jesus.
>
> Philippians 4:6-7

First, notice this verse is addressed to people who may be suffering from anxiety. It begins by saying, "Do not be anxious about anything." This truth is tailored for people who are at a time in life when they are susceptible to emotional difficulties.

It is good to give thanks to the LORD, to sing praises to your name, O Most High.
—PSALM 92:1

Secondly, we notice that we are commanded to pray (read: "abide in the Lord") with an attitude of thanksgiving. We will learn in a moment how to have this kind of attitude.

Now here is the exciting part. Notice what happens when an anxious person abides in the Lord with an attitude of thanksgiving. The Lord gives that person something. See if you can find it in the two verses above.

THANKFULNESS — GOD'S WONDER DRUG

The Lord Gives Peace

What is peace? As we saw in an earlier chapter, peace is the opposite of stress. However, in a more general sense, peace is the antidote to all of our emotional struggles. If you are depressed, you need some peace. If you are fearful, you need some peace. If you are stressed, you need some peace.

The peace God promises to those who abide with an attitude of thankfulness is not ordinary peace. The verses in Philippians tells us it is a peace which surpasses all understanding. This means it is a peace like no other peace. This is not the kind of peace and satisfaction that can come from circumstances. This is not the kind of peace that comes from being numbed by drugs. This is a special peace. This is a surpassing peace.

The apostle Paul, who wrote the Bible book of Philippians, used this same expression in the book of Ephesians. There he said the love of Christ was a love that surpassed our understanding. By that, he meant the love of Christ is a different kind of love, and not just different by degree. No other love compares to the love of Christ.

May the Lord of peace himself give you peace at all times in every way.
—2 THESS. 3:16

Likewise, here in Philippians we learn that no other peace compares to the peace God gives to those who abide with an attitude of thanksgiving.

Another great thing to see in these two verses is what this peace will do for us. Philippians 4:7 tells us this peace, which comes from God, will guard our hearts and minds.

This guard duty is exactly what we need! When we go through difficult times, when we are most susceptible to things such as depression, stress, anxiety, fear, and discouragement, what we need is something to guard and protect our minds and our hearts. The Bible says this peace will do exactly that.

Do you see now why I call thankfulness God's wonder drug?

Imagine an old-fashioned seesaw on a child's playground. One end of the seesaw is thankfulness. The opposite end of the seesaw represents our emotional struggles such as depression, stress, and anxiety. When thankfulness goes up, depression goes down. When thankfulness goes down, stress and anxiety go up.

It is time to get our seesaw tilted in the right direction.

Why is thankfulness so powerful?

The first reason thankfulness is so powerful is that it changes our perspective. It is our perspective on problems and situations that determine our emotional response. If a person is negative, bitter, and looking for a reason to be mad and angry, then he or she will find it. However, if another person in the same life situation is looking for a reason to be thankful, he or she will likely find that as well. The difference is not the situation; the difference is the perspective.

Personally, I can think of times when I have rolled out of bed in a bad mood. Perhaps I was frustrated at somebody or something or I had a sense of dread or fear concerning a pending problem. With that kind of attitude, every little conversation I have with anyone turns into a source of stress. I get mad at my wife for not putting the toothpaste back in its place. I am impatient with my children as they are getting ready in the morning. I am short with my assistant when she reminds me of something I forgot to do the previous day. What has happened is I have begun to go through my day looking for reasons to be miserable, and I have found them.

What if I would have made the choice to look for reasons to be thankful? Would it have made a difference in my attitude and emotions? Absolutely! I could have had an attitude of thankfulness for my wife and my daughters. I could have enjoyed my time with them in the morning. I could have been thankful that my assistant cared enough to remind me about something I had forgotten. Perhaps my entire emotional profile would have been different had I chosen to look for reasons to be thankful.

When we make that choice, the thankful choice, it will change our perspective on everything. That alone can make a powerful difference in our lives.

Diminishing Returns?

The second reason thankfulness is so powerful is that it is progressive. The more you look for things to be thankful for, the more things you will find, and the more you will want to look for more things. Thankfulness tends to have a snowball effect.

I read and hear a great amount of advice about how to help people overcome emotional struggles. And with most of it, if it has any good affect at all, the effect is diminishing. If you would measure the effectiveness of the advice on day one as 8, then on day two it might be 6, and on day ten it will likely be 2 at best.

I have read where experts talk about how to overcome depression by suggesting things like adding more or brighter lights to your work environment, or getting up earlier in the morning, or getting more sleep at night, or keeping a running list of your emotions, or squeezing some silly putty. Then these same experts will give testimonies of how people have followed these instructions and felt better. Could those testimonies be true? Might adding brighter light bulbs to the fixtures in your workspace really help you overcome depression?

When you learn how to make this thankfulness choice and you stick with it, you will be surprised at how much better you feel in one hour, but you will be astonished at how much better you feel in one year.

I suppose there are many things that could have a short-term effect on your mood. However, that kind of effect has a diminishing return. Three days after adding brighter light bulbs to your workspace, you will have adjusted, and you will not even notice. The truth is there are depressed people in the most well lit workspaces in the world! And there are joy-filled people even in the dark.

However, when a person chooses to be thankful and chooses to look for reasons to be thankful, the beneficial effect to his or her emotional health is not only long lasting but, it is increasing. When you learn how to make this thankfulness choice and you stick with it, you will be surprised at how much better you feel in one hour, but you will be astonished at how much better you feel in one year.

Thankful for What?

When I begin to talk about the power of thankfulness, sometimes people will respond by saying, "I don't have anything to be thankful for."

When someone says that, he betrays the fact that he does not really understand thankfulness. Thankfulness is not a feeling like happiness or hunger or pain. No. Thankfulness is a choice!

You can choose to be thankful. Try this little exercise.

What have you had to eat in the last three days? Are you thankful for that? No matter how meager your rations have been in the last few days, I bet you have eaten more and better than some of my friends on the coast of Kenya. Therefore, you can be thankful for something.

What is the comfort level of the place where you are now reading this book? I do not imagine anyone will ever read this book while he or she is on the verge of freezing to death or near the point of suffering a heat stroke. It is very unlikely that someone will be reading this book while stuck under a collapsed building following an earthquake or while trapped in the stairwell of a burning building. Therefore, you can be thankful for something else.

This may seem like an exercise in absurdity, but I am trying to demonstrate that no matter how bad your life situation is, there are some things you could choose to be thankful for. You cannot choose how you feel. You cannot choose whether your heart is broken. You cannot choose whether your head aches. You cannot choose whether you are tired. Nevertheless, you can choose whether you are thankful.

Some might say it would be easier to be thankful if I had more stuff to be thankful for. That is simply not true. There are people with much more stuff than you, who have a much easier life than you, who are also filled with bitterness and anger, and who do not have one thankful bone in their bodies. And, there are people whose station in life is much, much more difficult than yours but they have hearts overflowing with thanksgiving.

Again, thankfulness is not a feeling. Thankfulness is not tied to your situation in life. Thankfulness is in no way connected to circumstances. Thankfulness is a choice.

I Think I Am Thankful

Are you learning new things about thankfulness? Let me share another peculiarity about thankfulness that almost no one understands.

Thankfulness has no power unless it is expressed!

Most people think they are thankful, but many of them are wrong. You can only truly be thankful if you have expressed, and are expressing your thankfulness.

Let me give you an example which I often encounter in counseling sessions. A husband and a wife will come to see me because they are having difficulty in their marriage. At some point early in the counseling session I will look at the wife and say, "Tell me what the real problem is." Many times, she will then say that her husband is not thankful for anything she does. She will say he is not thankful for how she keeps the house, he is not thankful for how she washes his clothes, he is not thankful for how she takes care of the kids and prepares the meals. She will say he does not care about all of the sacrifices she makes to keep the marriage together and the kids taken care of.

Then I will look to the husband and say, "Is this true? Do you really not care? Are you really not thankful for all the things your wife does to make the household work?" I am sure you can guess what the ordinary reply of the husband is. He will say, "Of course I care, and of course I am thankful for all those things she does for me and for the family."

So what do you suppose the problem is? If the husband is genuinely thankful then why does the wife think he is not thankful? The easy answer is because he does not express his thankfulness. He does not tell her he is thankful. He does not treat her as if he were thankful. He does not tell the kids how thankful he is for the sacrifices of their mom. In no way is his thankfulness ever expressed. Therefore, his thankfulness has no power, and for all practical purposes, at least from his wife's perspective, he is not thankful.

Thankfulness has no power unless it is expressed!

What would you counsel this man to do? You would tell him to express his thankfulness, in word and in deed.

As simple as that, I have seen relationships mended and strengthened because the man chose to express the thankfulness that was always in his heart. What is the moral of the story? Thankfulness is not thankfulness unless it is expressed.

So, do you see why most people think they are thankful when in fact, they really are not? People tell me they are very thankful for all the things God has blessed them with; they are thankful for their families, for their health, for their friends, for their faith and for a thousand other things. I will then ask them when was the last time they specifically expressed that to the Lord. When was the last time you named the exact things you are thankful for as you either prayed to or focused on God? At that point, people usually give me a blank stare. Few people ever really express any real and specific thanksgiving to the Lord, and because of that, few people know the power that thankfulness can have in a person's life.

Are You the One or the Nine?

Let me show this to you through an interesting encounter Jesus had with ten men who had the dreaded disease of leprosy. We read in Luke 17 that the ten men were all in a group when they had an encounter with Jesus. They called out to Jesus and asked him to heal them of their leprosy. Jesus honored their request. All ten men were healed and told to go and show the authorities so that they could be officially recognized as healed.

I will thank you in the great congregation; in the mighty throng I will praise you.
—PSALM 35:18

After the ten completed the legal requirements to prove they no longer had the disease, one, and only one, of the ten came back to Jesus to express his thankfulness.

Jesus asked where the other nine were. Were they not also thankful? Jesus then proceeded to give a very special blessing (the gift of Salvation) to the one who was thankful.

Here is the important lesson I see in the story: Ten men were healed and only one returned to say so. If you had asked the nine who did not return if they were thankful, what would they have said? Of course, they would have claimed to be thankful! They had just been healed of the most dreaded disease of their day. They were thankful, but their thankfulness was silent. They were thankful, but only in their hearts. The contrast between the one and the nine is clear. Thankfulness only has real meaning and value if it is expressed.

Are you a thankful person? When was the last time you expressed your thankfulness? When was the last time you made a list of the reasons you were thankful for the blessings of God? Are you looking for things to be thankful for and ways to express that thankfulness? Do not underestimate the value of the wonder drug of expressed thankfulness!

Let us put this into practice now and begin to reap some of the immediate benefits of expressed thankfulness. Take a sheet of notebook paper and a pen, and go to a quiet place. In your quiet place, begin to write down everything for which you are thankful. If you get stuck in the first few minutes, then just begin to write down the very obvious things like the ability to take a breath and for the beating of your heart. Look around you for things to be thankful *When was the last time you expressed your thankfulness? When was the last time you made a list of the reasons you were thankful for the blessings of God?* for. Think about your family. Think about your past. Think about all that has happened in the past few weeks, months, and years.

Before long, you will be on a roll. Just keep writing. Fill up your page. Fill up the back of your page. Do not stop!

If you really did this activity, you have just experienced something wonderful. The thankfulness end of your seesaw just went sky high and the depression, stress, and anxiety end just went way down. Isn't that great. Thankfulness is a wonder drug!

How long will this change last? It will last as long as you remain thankful. It will last as long as you purposefully and specifically continue to express your thankfulness to the Lord. To keep this up all day and day after day is a learned skill. It will take some time and some practice. (The Lord will help.) At least you know now how it begins.

VINE DRESSIN(

1. Why do you think the Lord aims his most instructive verses (Philippians 4:6-7) on thankfulness specifically at people who are suffering from depression and anxiety?

2. Is thankfulness something you can choose to be? Why don't we choose to be thankful more often?

3. What are you thankful for?

4. We learned that thankfulness has no power unless it is expressed? When was the last time you expressed your specific thankfulness to your family and friends? How much time have you spent recently specifically thanking the Lord for his goodness and provisions?

CHAPTER 10

THE ROLE
OF MEDICINE

I should begin this chapter with the *disclaimer* that I am not a doctor. I do not have the license, education, or expertise to diagnose illnesses or prescribe medicine. This book is not about giving medical advice. This book and this chapter are about helping you see the truth about how to overcome stress, depression, and anxiety. And while these emotional struggles are often treated as medical issues in today's culture, I believe in most cases they are not, at least not primarily, thus the need for a book like this.

A *second disclaimer*: Please read this entire chapter before making any sort of decision or forming any new opinions about medication you may be taking to treat emotional or mental illness. An incomplete understanding of what I will show you in this chapter could lead to an incorrect decision.

Disclaimer number three: If you skipped to this chapter and are reading it first, you may find little that you agree with here. This chapter is written with the assumption that you have the new understanding of the nature and cause of emotional difficulties we have worked through in the preceding nine chapters.

Effective Drugs?

So what is the role of medicine in treating depression, stress, and anxiety? You do not have to look very hard to find evidence that people are turning to medications to treat their emotional and mental struggles more and more every day.

While emotional struggles are often treated as medical issues in today's culture, I believe in most cases they are not, at least not primarily, thus the need for a book like this.

A recent Reuters article by Health and Science Editor, Maggie Fox, states that in 2008, the number of antidepressant prescriptions written in the U.S. had risen to 164 million. That is a lot of medicine. That is a lot of depression.

So, has all of that expensive antidepressant medication with all of the scary potential side effects that come along with it improved the frequency or the severity of depression in America? The article says, no! The article goes on to quote Dr. Eric Caine of the University of Rochester in New York, who says, "There are no data to say the population is [mentally] healthier. Indeed, the suicide rate in the middle years of life has been climbing."

Well, despite the lack of solid evidence of the long-term effectiveness of this trend, more and more people are turning to prescription medications to treat mental ailments. There was a time in my counseling ministry when I would be surprised when someone told me they were taking antidepressants. Today, I am surprised when sometimes they tell me they are not taking antidepressants. It is not just that more people are taking the medicines, it is also that people are taking more and more of the medicines (sometimes two or three different kinds of antidepressants).

Worse than that, more and more young people, including teens and children, are taking the drugs. In fact, according to the Journal of the American Medical Association, the number of 2- to 4-year-olds on psychiatric drugs including antidepressants like Prozac jumped 50 percent between 1991 and 1995. That prestigious journal also confirmed that preschoolers seem to be leading the growth in the market for antidepressants.

Three Potential Problems

As I see it, there are three potential problems with using medication as the primary treatment for depression, stress, or anxiety. *First, the use of medication can sometimes undermine personal responsibility.* It is important when we have struggles such as depression that we dig down and find the root cause. We need to search and discover if there is something in our lives that we should remove or is there something not in our lives that we should add. Remember, pain is a good thing because it lets us know there is a problem that should be addressed. It is like the man who treats his recurring chest pain with a handful of aspirin. He is likely masking a problem that may one day kill him.

Often when people begin to treat their emotional pain with medication, they give up any kind of personal responsibility. They stop asking the hard questions. They stop trying to make changes. They become too reliant on the medication and end up robbing themselves of the opportunity for true emotional health.

The best illustration I can give you stems back to a problem I had with acid reflux a few years ago. The pain in my chest got worse and worse. So eventually, I went to see a doctor. She told me what was going on with my body and how this could become a very serious problem if it were not fixed.

Ok. So how do I fix it?

She said the primary cause was that I was overweight. If I would lose about thirty pounds, then I was much less likely to struggle with the acid reflux. She also prescribed a medicine that turned out to be effective in stopping the pain.

What I needed to do was use the medicine to control the problem while I focused on losing weight and getting my body healthy the right way. What I did instead was just take the medicine and not worry about my weight. In the short term, the medicine worked well. However, in the long term, it never really brought the real health and recovery I wanted and needed. Only in the last year have I learned my lesson and re-assumed personal responsibility for the health of my body. I am thankful for the medicine, but I am not thankful for how I allowed it to substitute for my personal responsibility.

The Real Goal?

The second problem with taking medications to treat emotional problems is that the medications provide a poor substitute for real emotional health. In a previous chapter, we learned what it means to have the fruit of the Spirit in your life. We talked about our need for real love, joy, peace, patience and so on. No pill will ever provide that. Sure, a pill may cover over the pain of depression or the nervousness of stress, and that may be important, but that is not the ultimate goal. The ultimate goal is emotional health. The ultimate goal is joy and peace! If you are expecting a pill to provide these, in the long run, you will be disappointed.

Drug Safety?

The third problem with most medications prescribed to treat depression or stress or anxiety is that the drugs are not nearly as effective or as safe as most people believe.

Through the years, there has always been someone who claimed to have a medical treatment for the cure of depression. In 1841, Abraham Lincoln submitted himself to Dr. Ansen Henry for treatment for his melancholy (depression). Henry was a strong proponent of the treatment method prescribed by the eminent physician, Dr. Benjamin Rush, who said the treatment should include, "direct and drastic interference with the patient's body and mind." He believed this was the best course of action because he thought, wrongly, that depression was caused by black bile in the abdomen. We cannot be certain about the specifics of Lincoln's medical care, but if Dr. Henry treated him as he treated his usual melancholy patients then the following are the things that would have happened.

First, Abraham Lincoln would have been bled out. Up to twelve and a half pints of blood would have been bled out of Lincoln's body in two weeks. (The average adult body contains 10-12 pints of blood.) Next, he would have been blistered by placing small, heated glass cups at the temples, behind the ears, and at the nape of the neck. (Sometimes leaches were used instead of the heated cups.) Then drugs would have been given to induce vomiting and diarrhea. The common drugs physicians used for this at that point in history were mercury (a deadly toxin), arsenic (a poison, used after World War I to make chemical weapons), and strychnine (rat poison).

Lincoln would have likely been forced to fast for days and then given large doses of ginger, black pepper and tar pills with water or peppermint tea. Painful mustard rubs would have been applied to his skin and then he would have been plunged into alternating hot and cold baths. Dr. Henry would know the treatment was working if, at the end of this horrible ordeal, Lincoln's stool had turned green. (I am not making this up.)

So after the good doctor had bled him, purged and puked him; starved him, dosed him with mercury, rat poison, and black pepper; rubbed him with mustard, and plunged him in cold water, did Lincoln's depression improve? What do you think?

History tells us two things: Lincoln's depression deepened, and he never went back to Dr. Henry for a second treatment.

I recently saw a television commercial for a new supplemental drug for depression. The spokesperson on the commercial asked, "Does your anti-depressant medicine not work for you? Then maybe you should talk to your doctor about adding our new supplemental anti-depressant pill."

As I listened to this question, my first thought was, if your anti-depressant medicine is not working maybe you should talk to your doctor about stop-taking the pill!

Dr. David Powlison, editor of the Journal of Biblical Counseling and author of many excellent books on the subject of depression and counseling, said this in an interview broadcast on Focus on the Family.

> *"According to the top end research, when the effects of modern anti-depressants are measured, it turns out that there is a twenty percent genuine psychoactive effect where the chemical makes people feel better. Sixty percent is a placebo effect, meaning that the person feeling better is a result of his or her faith or confidence in the pill, but it has nothing to do with the actual chemical compounds being ingested. And then there is a twenty percent highly deleterious or negative side effect."*

He went on to say that when you crunch the numbers, it is a wash. About twenty percent of people experience an actual drug induced positive result; about twenty percent experience a serious side effect. In light of this, my thinking is that this may not be the best way to try to find true emotional health. What do you think?

Chemical Imbalances?

Some people will say, "I thought depression, stress, and anxiety were caused by chemical imbalances in the body that need to be corrected."

The truth is there may be measurable chemical imbalances in the bodies of those who suffer from emotional distress. But it does not logically or necessarily follow that the imbalances cause the distress. The real question is, do the chemical imbalances cause someone to be depressed, does depression cause the chemical imbalances, or are both caused by some other influence? This is the problem with some of these statistics you hear. While the stats may be able to show that one thing correlates with another thing, that does not necessarily mean the first thing caused the second thing.

For instance, statistics show that generally people who own more books are better readers than people who own fewer books. Now, does this mean that owning more books makes you a better reader or could it be that being a better reader will likely lead you to buy more books? Which is the cause, and which is the result?

So which came first, the emotional distress or the chemical imbalances?

Ouside Stimuli

Another way to look at this same thing is to examine chemical imbalances and their relationship with outside stimuli. If you sit down and watch a very sad movie, you will likely be sad. You may be moved to tears. All kinds of chemical changes will happen in your body and these chemical changes will make salty water come out of your eyes. Now, I am not smart enough to understand or explain those chemical changes, but I do know this: The real source of your sadness is not the chemical changes inside your body. The source of your sadness is what is going on outside your body combined with your choice to sit and focus on it for 90 minutes. If you do not believe me, go rent a copy of the old Walt Disney movie *Old Yeller*, or Tri-Star's *Steel Magnolias*. I promise you those movies will lead to some chemical imbalances in your body that will predispose you to episodes of sadness.

The same is true if you watch a fast-paced thriller. You may feel your heart race. Your adrenaline (a mood altering hormone) may kick in. You feel different. However, the primary cause is what you have chosen to focus on, not some messed up blood or hormone chemistry.

In these scenarios, focus determined chemical changes, which in turn determined mood. Some would look at that and say our mood is determined by chemical changes. I would look at that and say our mood is determined by our focus.

Obviously, chemicals and hormones do play a part. Take for instance menstruation or a problem with the thyroid gland. Both of those situations will cause imbalances that will influence a person's temperament and mood. We could also look at the case of post-partum depression and its obvious connection with chemical and hormonal changes. Nevertheless, even those challenges, as real as they are, can often be moderated by the fruit of the Spirit at least as effectively as many medications.

The Proof Is In The Pudding

The bottom line is not who has the most persuasive argument or who has the most impressive credentials. The proof is in the pudding. It is the evidence that speaks the loudest.

What is the evidence? Medications have never provided real, long lasting emotional health. Drugs cannot give you love, joy, or peace. The fruit of the Spirit just works. The fruit of the Spirit defines authentic, enduring emotional health. As the Scripture teaches, the fruit of the Spirit is what every person desires in the deepest part of his or her heart.

The Role of Medicine

Does medicine have a role to play? I believe the answer is yes. There are two roles where medicine can be a great help.

First, medicine can sometimes provide temporary relief of severe symptoms of depression, stress, and anxiety while a person draws closer to the Lord and begins to bear spiritual fruit.

As I write this chapter, I am eight days away from running in my first marathon. I felt good about the upcoming run until six days ago when I developed a painful foot problem called Plantar Fasciitis. Last night a doctor friend took me to see a podiatrist friend of his. The podiatrist gave me some exercises and stretches that will help the tendon heal in a few months. In addition to that, he gave me a shot of cortisone to take away the pain for a couple weeks until the plantar fascia can begin to heal.

The cortisone is the temporary relief I needed today to relieve the symptoms. The stretching and exercises are what I need to regain health in my foot. I am thankful for the former today, but I will be grateful for the latter for a lifetime.

The second helpful use of medicine is in the unusual cases of some types of brain disorders. It is out of the scope of this book or my expertise to give much insight on such things as bipolar disorder, schizophrenia, paranoia, post-traumatic stress disorder, obsessive-compulsive disorder, etc.

To someone suffering from a disorder like one of these, I would say three things. First, do not ignore the fruit of the spirit. A close and fruit bearing relationship with God will make all of your burdens easier. Second, I have witnessed people who have experienced improvement with some of these challenges because of medicine. And that leads to my third comment: If you suffer from a disorder like one of these, then you should be under the care of a medical doctor.

> *Trust in the LORD with all your heart; do not depend on your own understanding. Seek his will in all you do, and he will show you which path to take.*
> —PROV. 3:5-6 NLT

To wrap this up, when it comes to using drugs to treat depression, stress, and anxiety, here are a few things to remember:

- Let your ultimate goal be emotional health, not merely symptom doping.

- Never stop taking prescribed drugs without talking to your doctor.

- Listen to your doctor; ask questions about the reasonable expectations of the benefits of the drugs that may be prescribed, and then do some research. Treat everything you read (including this book) with some healthy skepticism. Think for yourself.

- Lean on the wisdom of the Lord.

VINE DRESSING

1. How common do you think it is for people to use medication to treat depression, stress, or anxiety?

2. How effective do you think those drugs are in producing real joy and peace?

3. How can doping the pain of mental illness sometimes be a bad thing?

4. One-hundred fifty years after Abraham Lincoln was treated for depression with the best modern medicine had to offer, people read the story and think those doctors must have been crazy. What do you think they will be saying about today's modern treatments one-hundred years from now?

5. Some suggest that mental illnesses are a result of chemical imbalances. What could be another possible explanation for some of this correlation between chemical abnormalities and mental illness?

6. In your view, what should the role of medicine in the treatment of depression, stress, and anxiety be?

CHAPTER 11

ABIDING ON STEROIDS

In this book, you have learned how the key to overcoming emotional pain is to grow the fruit of the Spirit in your life. And you have also learned the key to growing the fruit of the Spirit in your life is abiding in Christ. So how can we push our abiding into overdrive? How can we fast track some of this fruit?

It is important to remember that fruit grows at its own pace. However, there is something you can do to help fruit mature as quickly as possible. That something is: *Scripture memorization.*

Perhaps this doesn't sound like very much fun to you and maybe it doesn't sound very helpful, but let me share some of the benefits of memorizing verses from God's word.

First, it helps us overcome temptation. It helps us to live free of sin. The Bible communicates this truth like this:

> I have stored up your word in my heart, that I might not sin against you.
>
> Psalm 119:11

The writer of this Psalm had learned this important lesson. The more of God's word we can learn and memorize, the better able we will be to overcome temptation and sin.

The best example of this is Jesus himself. Jesus went through a time of intense temptation. At each turn, Jesus responded to the temptation by quoting Scripture he had memorized. Jesus used memorized Scripture as a tool to resist the worst temptation. Since we have learned that nothing contributes to depression faster than sin, then memorization, if for no other reason, should be a great strategy to battle mental and emotional pain.

Whatever was written in former days was written for our instruction, that through endurance and through the encouragement of the Scriptures we might have hope.
—ROMANS 15:4

Another benefit of Scripture memorization is it provides us with a constant reminder of the promises of God. When we are in a difficult situation, sometimes we forget all of the ways God has promised to take care of us and to provide for us. Scripture memory gives us the assurance we need in the most difficult of times.

Memorizing Bible verses also helps us to learn and retain Bible knowledge. You can read a passage and think you have a good handle on what it means, but through the repetition required to memorize, the meaning of the verses become much deeper and richer. In addition, the lessons you learn from these verses stick in your heart and mind longer when they are memorized.

However, *the biggest benefit to us in Scripture memorization is it puts our abiding in Christ into hyper drive.*

If the best way to get close to Christ is through his word, then it makes sense that memorizing his word would make the relationship even closer. When we memorize we internalize his word. It becomes part of us and it leads to better abiding.

Let us review what we learned about abiding and God's word in the beginning. Here is what Jesus said in John 15:7:

> If you abide in me, and my words abide in you, ask whatever you wish, and it will be done for you.
>
> John 15:7

Do you see the connection between God's word and abiding?

Since he speaks to us and nourishes us through his word, when we can bring that word into our heart, then we can hear and be nourished on a more continual basis. Of course, the Holy Spirit is always with us and that is essential to abiding, but his word is also very important, and his word is not always with us unless we memorize it.

Look at this lesson Jesus taught:

> If you abide in my word, you are truly my disciples, and you will know the truth, and the truth will set you free.
>
> John 8:32

If we abide in his word, then the truth of the word will set us free! What better reason could there be for working hard to memorize Scripture.

But you are not sure you can do it. Isn't that what you are thinking? It is too hard. It takes too much time. I am too old. There is too much stuff running around in my brain.

Well, let me ask you a question. If I offered to give you $1,000 for every verse you could memorize in the next week, how many do you think you could learn? A bet you could learn at least one or two. For $1,000 per verse, I imagine you could learn a dozen or a dozen dozen. "But," you might say, "Nobody is offering to give me $1,000 per verse." You are correct, but read what the Bible says about the value of knowing and even memorizing Scripture:

> More to be desired are they than gold, even much fine gold; sweeter also than honey and drippings of the honeycomb. Moreover, by them is your servant warned; in keeping them there is great reward.
>
> Psalm 19:11

Therefore, it is really just a matter of how much you value God's word. It is simply about how badly you want to live a life characterized by the fruit of the Spirit.

Let me give you some simple steps to get you started.

First, have a plan. Nothing is ever really accomplished without a plan. There are plenty of Bible memorization plans available. There are books with the 100 verses every believer should know. Those are good. There is a website that lists *Fighter Verses*. These are lists of one verse per week you learn for five years. This is a very good list to start with. (Resources and links can be found at www.IlluminatingTheDarkness.com.) It does not matter what your plan is, but it matters that you have a plan. What is the old adage? If you fail to plan, then you plan to fail.

Second, know that a little bit, often, is better than much, seldom. Do you know what that means? You are much better learning one verse a week and working on that for a couple of minutes several times a day, than trying to learn a whole list of verses in one day. Pace yourself. A little bit at a time faithfully will pay great dividends in your life.

> *Memorize a verse a week for the next year, and your abiding in Christ will be producing more fruit than you imagined possible.*

Third, find some accountability. Find someone who will check on you. Maybe your spouse or a good friend will do this plan with you. The accountability will help you stick with your commitment. Accountability on something like this is essential. Do not start until someone has agreed to help you.

There you have it. Memorize a verse a week for the next year, and I promise your abiding in Christ will be producing more fruit than you imagined possible.

VINE DRESSING

1. How did Jesus use memorized Scripture to live a victorious life?

2. What would prevent you from memorizing one verse per week?

3. What is your Scripture memory plan?

4. Who can you partner with in this plan?

CHAPTER 12

WHAT NOW?

S o now, what should I do?
You are likely reading this book because you or someone you love is suffering from depression, stress, or anxiety, and you have come to a place of desperation. The good news is, if you have read this far in this book you now have a new perspective on the problem and new information on the solution. You know that emotional and mental health is possible and you know the path to get there.

Bad News

The bad news is, all of this information will probably do you no good. You may be surprised that, as the author of this book, I would write something like that, but it is true.

I hope I have not wasted your time, but the problem was never that you were not smart enough. And while the information and perspective revealed in this book is in all likelihood new to you, you were not depressed because you did not know certain information, and it will not go away now because you do.

No! Change comes, not from knowing, but from doing. If I have learned anything from my years of counseling and leading, it is this: *Information without application yields no transformation.* You will not be any better off for knowing the truths I have shared in this book, unless you embrace them and apply them to your daily life.

That is the good news (you have a new perspective and better information), the bad news (information alone brings no real change), and now the very good news: If you do adopt these principles into your life, you will know joy and peace like you have never known them before!

How should you get started?

The first step to any serious endeavor should be to write it down. This may seem like an elementary or meaningless exercise, but goals and objectives on paper are many times more powerful than goals and objectives in your head. Invest a little time, and write down your plan for your daily appointment with God. Write down when and where you are going to do this. Write down what fruits of the Spirit you hope to see bud and bloom first in your life. Write down a list of things you are thankful for. Write all of this down as if it were a letter to the Lord. Make this a written prayer.

Now read your prayer to the Lord. Ask him to help you. Ask him to help you stay consistent. Ask him to draw close to you over the next days and weeks. Ask him to bear fruit in your life, the fruit of the Spirit.

Remember, you will not be an expert at this appointment with God in the beginning. As I said, there is a learning curve. It takes time for the relationship to deepen. Soon, this will be second nature.

The next step is to find someone who can partner with you in this. The Bible says, "As iron sharpens iron, so a man sharpens the countenance of his friend" (Proverbs 27:17 NKJ). The word countenance refers to a person's mood, attitude, and emotional strength. "Sharpen your countenance" and "overcome depression" could mean precisely the same thing.

You need a friend who can encourage you when you need encouragement and push you when you need pushing. In fact, in the same chapter of the book of Proverbs, the Bible says, "Faithful are the wounds of a friend" (Proverbs 27:6). This accountability partner needs to be someone who loves you enough to hold your feet to the fire as you begin to transform your life. He should be someone who is not afraid to ask specific questions and give you some honest feedback.

Step 1: Write it down your plan and commitment!

Step 2: Find someone to hold you accountable.

It would be very helpful if your accountability partner read this book. Let him or her take your copy for a week. Ask your friend to read at least the first twelve chapters so there will be an understanding of what you are trying to accomplish. Together you can grow and enjoy the sweet fruit of the Spirit.

Now, let us do a quick survey of the ground we have covered. As we go through this, if there is anything unclear to you, stop reading there, go back, and review that chapter. All of these pieces are necessary to make this work.

What Have We Learned?

We began by learning that a life of persistent depression, stress, and anxiety is not normal. It is not normal in the sense that it is not the way normal life should be. There is a path to improvement. There is a better way to live. You can overcome this emotional pain.

Next, we learned that emotional struggles such as depression and stress are not really the problem. They feel like the problem, but in reality they are only symptoms of the real problem, just like pain in your side can be a symptom of a greater problem in your body. Therefore, in some sense we should be thankful for pain, all pain, because it directs us to a problem we can work to resolve.

Then we learned the slightly more difficult to understand principle that teaches us that something like depression is not something that is wrong in us. Rather, depression is the absence of something right in us. In this case, what we lack is joy. Moreover, just as darkness disappears when light enters the scene, so depression vanishes when joy finds its way in. We learned that the same is true with all emotional pain. Worry fades when patience shines in. Stress is displaced by peace. Strife is overcome by love.

Eureka! At last, we discovered the fruit of the Spirit. We learned that this special fruit comes in nine varieties, and those nine varieties or categories describe what it would be like to have perfect mental and emotional health. We learned that the right goal in life is not to numb our depression or bury our stress. The right goal is to vanquish our depression with joy and displace our stress with peace.

So we began to search for the source of this special fruit. The Bible taught us that it is the fruit *of* the Spirit. It comes from the Spirit of God. In fact, the Bible tells us that to grow the fruit of the Spirit in our lives we must be connected to the vine of the Lord. Apart from that connection, there will never be any genuine, lasting, sweet, mature fruit in our lives.

This connection to the Lord has two parts: We must be connected, and we must remain connected. Both are required if we are going to grow any fruit. The Bible word for getting connected is salvation. The Bible word for remaining connected is abiding.

In chapter four, we learned the specifics of getting connected. Beginning in chapter five, we learned the specifics of remaining connected.

To remain connected involves building on the personal and daily relationship you have with the Lord. The first tool we use to do that is a daily appointment with him. In this appointment, through Bible study and prayer, your relationship with God matures and strengthens. We learned not only the how-to of this daily time, but also the four key factors in making this time most valuable. Those four elements are time, passion, consistency, and compounding.

The second tool for relationship building is focus. We learned how our focus determines much of our emotional state. If our focus is on the Lord and abiding in him, then we are likely to experience and enjoy the fruit of the Spirit in our lives: Love, joy, peace, patience, etc. We learned a number of strategies to help us keep our focus on the Lord throughout the day.

Next, we discovered how to kick abiding into high gear with something called thankfulness. We learned several biblical truths about thankfulness like how it is the channel through which the Lord gives us real peace, how it is progressively more powerful hour by hour and day by day, and how most people nullify all this power because they do not know one simple truth about thankfulness. What is that simple truth? Thankfulness is not thankfulness unless it is expressed.

In the next chapter we looked at the role of medicine in the fight for mental and emotional health. We learned how much of what is said about the cause and effect of chemical imbalances in the body is logically suspect. Then, armed with that information, we discussed the limits of what medications can do and what their proper purpose should be in the treatment of mental illness in otherwise healthy people.

Finally we learned how the simple act of memorizing Scripture can spur the growth of the fruit of the Spirit in our lives. While few people find this an easy task, everyone who makes the effort is rewarded with lasting fruit.

Where do the next chapters take us?

While the first part of this book was all about a comprehensive strategy to find emotional health, the last half of this book is about specific tactics to tackle specific issues. I have called this section, "Slaying Emotional Dragons" because sometimes even while we are closely abiding in the Lord, there will be some personal battles with emotional pain that need to be addressed very specifically.

The primary reason we struggle with depression instead of experiencing joy and have stress rather than peace is a lack of the fruit of the Spirit. But there can be some other causes as well. It is important to remember the specific strategies will have their maximum effect only in the lives of those who are abiding in Christ and enjoying the fruit of the Spirit. These are secondary treatments and will not give you the baseline of love, joy, and peace that you need first and that you can only find in the fruit.

In fact, if you try to apply these lessons without first seeking the fruit of the Spirit you may be very discouraged by the instructions I give and the results they have. For instance, in the "Slaying Emotional Dragons" chapter on depression, I am going to suggest a possible cause for depression and then share a remedy. If you start with that chapter instead of first focusing on bearing the fruit of the Spirit, you may think to yourself, "That is not what is causing my depression!" And, you will probably be right. Most depression

> *The primary reason we struggle with depression instead of experiencing joy and have stress rather than peace is a lack of the fruit of the Spirit. But there can be some other causes as well.*

is not caused by what I will share with you in that chapter. Most depression is the result of a lack of the fruit of the Spirit, especially the fruit of joy. The depression chapter is only for those who are abiding in Christ and experiencing the fruit, but still struggling with this particular emotional problem.

So remember, the hope is in abiding in the Lord! Nevertheless, I do believe these last chapters will help you overcome some humps in your journey to mental and emotional health with some specific strategies from God's word.

So, are you ready to experience and enjoy the fruit of the Spirit? Let the journey begin!

VINE DRESSING

1. In this chapter we were reminded that it isn't more information that will make a difference in your emotional health, rather it is action. What is your plan to put what you have learned into action?

2. When are you going to start?

3. What are your goals? What are your expectations?

4. Who can partner with you in this new endeavor to abide with the Lord? Who can help hold you accountable?

CHAPTER 13

AFTERWORD

I spoke at a special funeral today. In fact, I speak at many funerals, but today was very different. This was the memorial service for Gordon B. Dolloff. Gordon was 89 years old. In the front row was June, his wife of 65 years. June was flanked on both sides by her children and their children. If I could somehow show you a photograph of the service, you would notice nothing out of the ordinary. But ask anyone who there; this was no ordinary memorial service.

Gordon suffered much in the last decade. He was a victim of Parkinson's disease, and the disease had taken its toll on his body. His arms constantly shook; his frame was weak; his voice could not get above a whisper. In addition to all of this were the normal trials and difficulties that come with living well into your 80's. It was time for Gordon to go home, to go to his heavenly home.

So what made this funeral so different? It was Gordon. Gordon was different. What was so different about Gordon was his *joy*. Through every difficulty, through every fall, through every trip to the hospital, through every stint in the nursing home for rehab, Gordon was exactly the same. He was filled with joy. In fact, even when his life was particularly arduous, he could have been the universal spokesperson for the fruit of the Spirit. He nailed every aspect of the fruit: Love, joy, peace, patience, kindness, goodness, faithfulness, gentleness, and self-control.

One by one, for nearly an hour, people came to the podium or stood at their seats and shared the secret to Gordon's unceasing joy.

I can remember seeing Gordon come in the door for Sunday worship when it was ten degrees outside with ice and snow on the ground. He would be barely able to stand with a walker. I would tell him good morning, and he would begin to talk to me. He was so weak, the only way I could hear his voice was to stoop down with my ear inches from his face. What would he be saying? He would be trying to encourage *me*. He would tell me to be strong in the Lord. He would tell me how good the Lord had been to him in the last week. He would tell me how he had spent time praying for any hardships I might be facing. And he would quote Scripture. Gordon was one of a kind!

So the funeral consisted of me and another pastor on our staff sharing a few words. There was good heartfelt singing of some old classic hymns. All of that was pretty ordinary, but then I gave his family and friends an opportunity to say something. One by one, for nearly an hour, people came to the podium or stood at their seats and shared the secret to Gordon's unceasing joy. What did they share? They told the story of the first twelve chapters of this book!

His family talked about how he spent time daily studying the Bible. They spoke of his earnest commitment to prayer. They shared about his life-long passion to memorize as much of the Bible as he could possible fit in his mind. After his family spoke, his friends stood to speak. They told the same story. Anecdote after anecdote of how difficult circumstances in his life did nothing but shine the spotlight on his joy. Friends talked especially about his heart for prayer and his passion for God's word and how that had impacted them. No one used the phrase, *abide in Christ*, but they presented a picture of someone who knew exactly what it meant and someone who strived to abide every day.

I didn't need any confirmation that abiding in Christ yields the fruit of the Spirit. I know it does because of my personal experience, the experiences hundreds of others have shared with me through the years, and of course the testimony of Scripture. I didn't need confirmation, but I got it anyway!

Thank you Lord that the fruit of the Spirit can be a reality in the life of every person who abides in you, regardless of one's circumstances. Thank you Lord that the fruit doesn't diminish over time, but only matures and sweetens. Thank you Lord for the fact that even if we lose everything else in life, the fruit will remain. Thank you Lord for such a timely confirmation!

SLAYING EMOTIONAL DRAGONS

WORRY/ANXIETY

Caution: If you have flipped to back of this book to read about strategies for specific problems, then you are making a mistake. Without first understanding the material presented in the first ten chapters of this book, you will find this chapter confusing, controversial, and unsatisfying. Please read the first chapters first.

Do you continue to struggle with worry and anxiety even now that the fruit of the Spirit is growing in your life? Has anxiety not faded as the fruit has budded? Often anxiety can be hard to escape from. People can sometimes become overwhelmed with a problem or the fear of a problem to the point where normal living is impossible. Symptoms can range from mild distraction to a person being so consumed with the problem that he or she cannot sleep, eat, work, or even carry on a normal conversation.

Worry is not an insignificant thing. It is very serious, and it can be very debilitating. There are a myriad of medical problems that have worry as one of their causes. Worry has been connected with everything from nausea to ulcers and obesity to heart disease. Sometimes you hear people say they are "worried sick" or they were nearly "worried to death." As it turns out, medical science suggests there may be more truth to those statements than we realize.

The good news is, worry can be overcome! You do not have to live with the terrible, heavy weight of anxiety. Peace is possible.

How do we know this? Let us turn to the Bible. The Lord gives us assurance of peace in two ways: first through promises, and then more importantly, through commands.

Promises

There are scores of promises in the pages of the Bible that give us hope in the face of worry. To list and discuss all of them would require a stack of books. However, let me share a few verses with you.

> Cast your burden on the Lord, and he will sustain you;
> he will never permit the righteous to be moved.
> > Psalm 55:22

> In the multitude of my anxieties within me, Your comforts delight my soul.
> > Psalm 94:19

> Blessed is the man who trusts in the Lord, whose trust
> is the Lord. He is like a tree planted by water, that sends
> out its roots by the stream, and does not fear when heat
> comes, for its leaves remain green, and is not anxious in
> the year of drought, for it does not cease to bear fruit.
>
> Jeremiah 17:8

> Even though I walk through the valley of the shadow
> of death, I will fear no evil, for you are with me; your
> rod and your staff, they comfort me.
>
> Psalm 23:4

Do those verses bring comfort? Do they dispel your anxiety? Honestly, they probably do not. You may not even have read them very closely, if at all. The promises of the Lord sometimes ring hollow in the ears of those suffering the most. While these promises are certainly true, they seem to have more potency in keeping us from worry than in rescuing us from it. Therefore, if you are not suffering from anxiety, I encourage you to incorporate those verses and others like them into your life through reading and memorizing. You will find great value in doing so. However, if you are stuck in the tentacles of full-blown anxiety, stay with me as we focus on the encouragement and instruction we gain from the Bible's commands about worry.

Commands

When the Lord gives us a command, there is always an implied promise inside the command. The promise is that the subject of the command is achievable. Let me explain. When I tell my two young daughters to clean their rooms or do their laundry before bedtime, implicit in that command is my belief that they are capable of doing it. I would never look at my youngest daughter and command her to rebuild the great pyramids of Egypt before she went to bed. That would be ridiculous. I obviously do not believe she is capable of doing that.

So, here is the relevant point. If the Lord gives us a command to do something in the Bible, we know we can do it! That is a valuable understanding. In fact, I believe the most helpful promises in the Bible are hidden in the commands of Scripture.

What commands does the Lord give us about worry and anxiety? Let us start with the simplest and most straight forward:

> I tell you, do not be anxious.
>
> Matthew 6:25

There is more to the verse than that, but let us just stop here for a moment and see what we can learn. Do you recognize the promise hidden in this command? In this command, we learn it is possible, reasonable, and practical to believe that we can "not worry." If worry has become a permanent fixture in your life, this is good news. There is hope.

The next seven and a half verses tell us how to accomplish this imperative.

> I tell you, do not be anxious about your life, what you
> will eat or what you will drink, nor about your body,

what you will put on. Is not life more than food, and the body more than clothing? Look at the birds of the air: they neither sow nor reap nor gather into barns, and yet your heavenly Father feeds them. Are you not of more value than they? And which of you by being anxious can add a single hour to his span of life?

And why are you anxious about clothing? Consider the lilies of the field, how they grow: they neither toil nor spin, yet I tell you, even Solomon in all his glory was not arrayed like one of these. But if God so clothes the grass of the field, which today is alive and tomorrow is thrown into the oven, will he not much more clothe you, O you of little faith?

Therefore do not be anxious, saying, 'What shall we eat?' or 'What shall we drink?' or 'What shall we wear?' For the Gentiles seek after all these things, and your heavenly Father knows that you need them all.

Matthew 6:25-32

Let us learn two essential lessons from these verses. For the first lesson, do this brief activity: Think about your largest source of worry and anxiety. What is the biggest problem you fear? Now take sixty seconds, and really focus on the problem. Think about how bad it is and how much worse it may be in the days to come. Brood over it for a full minute.

OK, time is up. You just spent one solid minute in intense worry. Did that help you? Did that bring a resolution to the problem? Do you feel better now? No! The first thing we learn from these verses is that worry does no good. There is no benefit in worrying.

In the middle of the passage above Jesus asks, "Which of you by worrying can add one cubit to his stature?" A cubit is the distance from your elbow to the tip of your middle finger, about a foot and a half. The question is meant, of course, to be rhetorical. Your worrying about an upcoming problem or potential problem will be about as useful as trying to add eighteen inches to your height by the force of your mind. Worry is unproductive when it comes to problem solving or mood lifting.

The next thing we learn is even more important. We learn that anxiety is the opposite of trust.

In these verses Jesus said, "Your heavenly Father knows that you need all these things." The Bible

Anxiety is the opposite of trust.

promises us that God knows what we need. He knows our life situations. He knows our weaknesses and our vulnerabilities. And he promises to meet our needs.

Therefore, when we worry, we are actually denying the promises of the Lord. That is why some have called worry, *temporary atheism*. While we are overwhelmed with worry, we are not trusting and believing in an all-powerful, all-knowing, all-loving God. Perhaps the phrase, *temporary atheism*, is a little harsh, but it does highlight the role of trust when it comes to anxiety.

When I give in to the temptation to worry, my choice is saying one of three things. Either I do not believe the Lord knows how to meet my needs, or I do not believe he is powerful enough to meet my needs, or I do not think he will be true to his promise to meet my needs.

Did you notice how the verses described the carefree spirit of the birds of the air and the lilies of the field? Wild animals and plants do not worry, so why should we worry about whether the Lord will care for us, especially in the light of the fact that we have been made in the image of God and forgiven through the sacrifice of his Son.

Therefore, worry and trust are mutually exclusive. They are opposites. When your worry is up, you know your trust is down. So, if we could somehow raise our level of trust, we would see worry disappear. Do you remember the seesaw analogy from the chapter on thankfulness? The same applies here. Worry and trust are on opposite ends of the same seesaw. They are never both up, and they are never both down. And herein lies the key to overcoming worry.

How To Raise Your Trust

What do we do to raise our level of trust?

The Bible gives some specific and practical instructions a few pages further into the New Testament. We will get there, but first let us finish studying the passage we started reading earlier. In the next and final verse, Jesus says:

> Seek first the kingdom of God and his righteousness,
> and all these things will be added to you.
>
> Matthew 6:33

Jesus teaches us the key to having this worry-banishing trust is to seek his kingdom and his righteousness. If this sounds a lot like the *Fruit-of-the-Spirit* and *abiding* principles we learned earlier, then that's good. You are getting the hang of this. Now let us continue to follow this line of reasoning and see how to increase our trust in a practical way, and thereby decrease our worry.

We find these practical instructions in the book of Philippians. We read these verses earlier, but let us read them again and learn something more.

> Do not be anxious about anything, but in everything by prayer and supplication with thanksgiving let your requests be made known to God. And the peace of God, which surpasses all understanding, will guard your hearts and your minds in Christ Jesus.
>
> Finally, brothers, whatever is true, whatever is honorable, whatever is just, whatever is pure, whatever is lovely, whatever is commendable, if there is any excellence, if there is anything worthy of praise, think about these things. What you have learned and received and heard and seen in me—practice these things, and the God of peace will be with you.
>
> Philippians 4:6-9

The writer of Philippians says that instead of worrying, we should do two things: pray and ponder. Those are the key action steps, but before we learn those, let us see what the real benefits will be.

In the middle of the passage we read, "The peace of God, which surpasses all understanding, will guard your hearts and minds in Christ Jesus" (Philippians 4:7).

All of this passage is focused on the subject of worry. So here we learn that if we do the action steps given in this passage, then the benefit is that our worry will be replaced with peace. Good news? Absolutely!

As we read this passage closely, we also learn two things about peace. First, it guards the heart and mind. The phrase *heart and mind* references the whole of our mental and emotional health. We learn that the peace of God can stand like a well-armed soldier guarding this aspect of our health. In my imagination, I picture the guards at the tomb of the Unknown Soldier in Arlington Cemetery. I can see the well-trained, well-armed soldier, ever watching, ever ready... guarding something precious to America. I know the peace of God is guarding my heart and mind in the same way.

You keep him in perfect peace whose mind is stayed on you, because he trusts in you.
—ISAIAH 26:3

Peace I leave with you; my peace I give to you. Not as the world gives do I give to you. Let not your hearts be troubled, neither let them be afraid.
—JOHN 14:27

This verse also tells us this peace is a peace that surpasses all understanding. It transcends human intellectual powers, human analysis, human insights, and human understanding. Because its source is the God whose judgments are unsearchable and whose ways are unfathomable, it is superior to human scheming, human devices, and human solutions.

Have you ever known anyone who exhibited a calm peace in the midst of life's worst storms? I have known people like that. Things could be falling apart all around them, but they seem to have a trust that cannot be shaken, a strength that could not be explained. How is that? It is due to the peace that surpasses understanding!

So, those are some great benefits. How can they be mine? Pray and Ponder! How do we pray and ponder? What do those words mean? Good questions. Let us focus first on prayer.

Prayer

Look back at how our focus passage begins:

> Do not be anxious about anything, but in everything
> by prayer and supplication with thanksgiving let your
> requests be made known to God.
>
> Philippians 4:6

Notice some very practical counsel about prayer. First, we are to pray about everything! If anything is big enough to tempt you to be anxious, then it is big enough to be the subject of your prayers. The verse emphasizes this by using the contrasting words "nothing" and "everything." Go back and see how those two words are used in Philippians 4:6. Should we be anxious about anything? No. Instead we should pray in everything. We are to trade our anxieties in for prayer. More on why this works in a moment, but let us decipher the rest of the verse.

The verse gives us the command to be in prayer, and then it talks about supplication. What is supplication? Simply put, supplication is another way to say "prayer." Now hold that thought, and let us look at the next part of the verse. It says to do this with thanksgiving. What is thanksgiving? Thanksgiving is expressing our thanks to the Lord through prayer. So in essence, thanksgiving is prayer. OK, the next verse says to let your requests be made known to God. What is that? It is prayer. Therefore, if we put all of these definitions together and do a little word substitution, here is what we come up with for the verse:

Be anxious for nothing, but in everything by prayer and
prayer, with prayer, pray!

This is not simplifying things too much. Instead of embracing anxiety or worry, we are to pray!

When a problem, a fear, or an obstacle come up in our lives, we should immediately begin to talk to the Lord about that. We should talk with him about our fears. We should talk about the different possibilities we see, the good possibilities and the bad possibilities. We should talk about how we should handle this. We should talk about it until we begin to feel some peace and assurance of God's power and love.

We should continue to pray daily about the issue until it is resolved or the issue passes. If fear or worry creep back into our minds, we should pray even more. Always remember that prayer is the way we stretch and exercise our trust; and trust is the antidote to worry.

Notice also, that Philippians 4:6 tells us to pray with thanksgiving. That means we should pray with a focus on how God has been faithful to us in the past. As I ask God for help with my fears of the future, I should also thank him for how he has already helped me through the challenges I have faced in the past.

I am praying now about some future obstacles I will face in my ministry. I have some unanswered questions. It would be easy for me to worry or have some fear of the future. As I have been praying about those obstacles, I have also been very careful to talk with the Lord about how he has faithfully provided for me in my ministry in the past. Those real life stories I express to God as prayers of thanksgiving become pure gold nuggets of peace that God pours back into my heart. Worry diminishes as I pray with thanksgiving!

Do you know the Bible story of David and Goliath? David was the unlikely opponent of the Old Testament's famous giant. All of the other men in the army of Israel, even the king of Israel, were afraid to fight him, but David was not. Do you remember what helped David overcome his fear and his anxiety? David said he remembered how the Lord had helped him defeat the lion and the bear. The memories of how the Lord had helped him before, banished his worry and allowed him to do the impossible.

Ponder

The word, ponder, means to give careful and focused thought to something. It means to consider something deeply and thoroughly. The bible tells us what we should ponder in Philippians 4.

> Whatever is true, whatever is honorable, whatever is just, whatever is pure, whatever is lovely, whatever is commendable, if there is any excellence, if there is anything worthy of praise, think about these things. What you have learned and received and heard and seen in me—practice these things, and the God of peace will be with you.
>
> Philippians 4:8-9

To describe pondering, this passage uses the verb "meditate." This is not some mystical exercise that involves sitting

Indian style and smelling incense. It simply means *to think*. This part of the Bible was originally written in the Greek language, and the original Greek word used here is the word from which we get our word logic. There is nothing mystical or super-spiritual about this. We are simply commanded to put our focus on certain things. We are to think on certain things.

Why is this important? It is because our outlook is determined by our focus.

I remember when I was learning to drive. I was terrible behind the wheel. My problem came because I was trying to get my head in such a position that I could line up the hood ornament (it was a long time ago) with the yellow stripe on the side of the road. That did not work. As I focused on the yellow stripe, the car was constantly drifting in that direction. Then my driver's education instructor told me to look up and focus on where I wanted the car to go. Wow. What a difference that made. If I focused on the side of the road, it was hard to stay in the middle of the road, but when I changed my focus to the long stretch of highway ahead of me, driving became a cinch.

The key to many things in life is our focus, and when it comes to worry and anxiety, this is especially true. If you focus on your problems and fears and ignore everything else going on in and around you, then your worry will get worse and worse. You will spiral into a sea of despair. These verses tell us to lift up our heads and begin to focus on some good things; focus on the right things.

How many people reading this book have created their own storm of desperation because they have been too focused on the wrong things?

I am reminded of the Mother Goose rhyme:

For every ailment under the sun, there is a remedy or there is none. If there be one, try to find it. If there be none, never mind it.

Now, some readers are thinking, "It is impractical to just ask me to drop my worry. I cannot drop it. It has a hold on me." You are right in thinking it would be impossible to just drop it or remove it from your mind. That is why this passage is so powerful. Let me show you what I mean.

What does Philippians 4:8-9 say I should focus on?

- Whatever things are true…
- Whatever things are noble…
- Whatever things are just…
- Whatever things are pure…
- Whatever things are lovely…
- Whatever things are of good report…
- Anything of virtue…
- Anything praiseworthy…

Will that really help dispel my anxiety? Yes, it will!

How to Get the Air out of a Mug

Do you know how to get all of the air out of a coffee mug? That is both a very difficult and a very easy problem to solve. It is difficult if your strategy is to suck out the air. In fact, it is a practical impossibility. Perhaps you could invent some sort of machine that would attach to the mouth of the mug and create a vacuum strong enough to get most of the air particles out without causing the mug to collapse, but it would take a herculean effort, and as soon as you removed the apparatus from the mug, the air would just go right back in.

That is a pretty good picture of someone who is trying to get the worry out of his or her heart and mind by just stopping. I have heard some people give that counsel. They have said, if worry is driving you mad, then just stop it. The problem is, that is practically impossible.

Let us go back to our coffee mug. What is the easy way to get the air out of the mug? Just fill it with coffee. As the coffee goes in, the air goes out. Fill it to overflowing, and you have successfully removed the air from the cup. How do we get worry out of our lives? Just fill our lives to overflowing with praying and pondering. Pray as if your life depended on it, and focus on whatever things are true, noble, just, pure, lovely and of good report. The more you do this, the more worry will leave you.

Practically Speaking

Practically speaking, how do we do this? How do we focus on things described in that list?

There is no one way that will fit everyone, but here are some suggestions:

- *Read the Bible.* Take an hour of free time and read through some of the Psalms. Do this every day that worry is an issue.

- *Read a Christian book.* There are many great Christian books, both fiction and non-fiction, that will help you focus on those things which are noble and true.

- *Listen to Christian music.* Some people are wired to gain encouragement through music. If you are one of those people, surround yourself with some good Christian music that you will enjoy.

- *Spend time with positive, encouraging Christian friends.* Did you know that in some ways mental and emotional health or illness is contagious? I do not mean there is a bug you can catch, but if you are around people who are focusing on whatever is true, noble, just, pure, lovely and of good report, that will rub off on you. If you hang out with people who focus on the opposite, that will rub off on you as well.

- *Spend time serving the Lord by serving others.* Nothing gets your spiritual blood flowing through your spiritual heart like hard working service and sacrifice. Find a ministry. Find a service project. Find someone you can help.

Certainly, there are many other ways to do this. The key is to continue to pray and ponder until your cup runs over and worry is gone.

Look back at how our verses began, "Be anxious for nothing, but in everything by prayer and supplication..." The Bible commands us to trade our anxiety in for prayer and pondering. Are you ready to give it a try?

VINE DRESSING

1. What are some of the medical issues that worry can contribute to?

2. The Bible contains many promises from the Lord. What role can these play in helping conquer worry and anxiety?

3. Is it possible to simply stop worrying? How does the Bible say we can accomplish this seemingly impossible feat?

4. What is the relationship between worry and trust?

5. What should be our first course of action when we begin to be overwhelmed with worry?

6. What are some practical strategies to help us ponder on the right things in the midst of worry and anxiety?

CHAPTER 14

SLAYING EMOTIONAL DRAGONS
STRESS

Caution: If you have flipped to back of this book to read about strategies for specific problems, then you are making a mistake. Without first understanding the material presented in the first ten chapters of this book, you will find this chapter confusing, controversial, and unsatisfying. Please read the first chapters first.

It seems everyone is familiar with the strains of stress. For some, stress is an aggravator that adds to the difficulty of day-to-day life. For others, stress is a crushing weight that prevents them from functioning normally and enjoying life. The good news is that the Lord wants you to live, not with stress, but with peace. He encourages us in Scripture with promises like this:

May the Lord of peace himself give you peace at all times in every way. The Lord be with you all.

2 Thessalonians 3:16

This verse teaches that peace is an attribute of God. God is never stressed. God never fears. God is never indecisive. And it is out of the very heart of who God is that he gives us peace. Peace is a gift. You can see this in the simple word "give." The word "give" implies a gift. Peace is God's gift to his children. Notice the verse also says he will give it "always in every way." This means this peace is not a passing peace or a haphazard peace. The Lord desires that we live with constant peace, regardless of our circumstances.

Stress is a killer of good health. Doctors have linked many very serious illnesses to stress. From ulcers to heart disease, there are numerous reasons to stress over stress.

So we know it is the Lord's desire that we have peace, but for most of us, peace is not our reality. Stress, more often than peace, is the theme of most people's lives. That is not good.

Stress can cause many problems. For one, stress is the worm eating away at the fruit of the Spirit. It is both an indicator that the fruit is not mature in a person's life and it is a destroyer of the fruit already there. It is hard to have love, joy, peace, patience, kindness and so on when we are under the heavy burden of stress.

Stress is also a killer of good health. Doctors have linked many very serious illnesses to stress. From ulcers to heart disease, there are numerous reasons to stress over stress.

Stress can also hurt relationships, including marriages. It can weaken our resistance to temptation. In addition, it can stop up our spiritual ears and blind our spiritual eyes from hearing and seeing what God has to teach us.

Cause of Stress

So what causes stress? Aside from a simple absence of the fruit of the Spirit (see the first half of this book), stress is most often the result of us getting outside of the boundaries God has given us for wise living. Have you ever ridden in a car with someone who was driving too fast? Did his driving introduce stress into your life? You have an idea of what you think is a safe speed to drive given traffic and road conditions. When the driver goes beyond that boundary, you begin to feel stress. Stress is the result of crossing boundaries.

Stress is the result of us getting outside of the boundaries God has given us for wise living.

We can think of many life examples of this truth. With your level of income and your obligations and responsibilities, there is a wise amount of money you should spend each month. When your expenses exceed that, what happens? You stress over your finances.

There is an amount of work that is reasonable and wise for a person to do. If you feel an obligation to do more than that, and to exceed that boundary, you will feel stress.

There is a reasonable amount of noise and commotion your kids should make at the end of your hard day of work. When their commotion surpasses that level, you are stressed.

Therefore, stress comes from the breaking of boundaries. However, there is more to stress than just that. Stress is amplified when we are breaking boundaries without a caring companion in the struggle. When we feel like no one knows or no one cares about the stress we are feeling then it is multiplied. When someone comes along side us and helps carry the load, or at least acknowledges the burden, it becomes much easier.

The Solution for Stress

OK, now that we have defined it, is there hope? Yes. There is a way to overcome stress and replace it with peace. There is a solution!

The simplest expression of this is found in the Bible book of 1 Peter.

> Humble yourselves, therefore, under the mighty hand of God so that at the proper time he may exalt you, casting all your anxieties on him, because he cares for you.
>
> 1 Peter 5:6-7

That is a short and simple passage, but it contains pure gold truths for those struggling with stress. Let us take a close look at it a phrase at a time.

It begins by instructing us to humble ourselves. Humility is not a very popular subject in our day. If you were to go into the self-help section of a major bookstore, you would find literally hundreds of books on how to improve yourself. There would be books on how to be successful and happy. There would be books on how to beat stress and depression. However, you would find no books on how to be humble. It is not something most Americans aspire to. Nevertheless, there is power in humility, as we will see by the time we get to the end of this chapter.

So how can I be humble? The first thing you must do is to understand who you are and who God is. This passage talks about the "mighty hand of God," which reminds us of God's power, knowledge, and authority. He is the one in control of everything. You and I are the ones in control of very, very little. He is the one who knows the future. You and I are the ones who are surprised all of the time. He is the one who can do anything without breaking a sweat. You and I are the ones who are tired after doing the laundry. If there is hope for the future, that hope rests with the God who is sovereign, not with you or me.

Understanding this truth is the beginning of humility. Now add to that understanding a little bit of trust and some submission, and we are there.

Who and how should we trust? We should trust the Lord. Specifically, we should trust his sovereignty, how he is ultimately in control of everything. Moreover, we should trust his goodness, how he loves us and wants what is best for us. That logically follows our understanding of who he is and who we are.

Submission is a little more difficult, but not any less important. Submission simply means we quit fighting the Lord and we quit fighting life, and we just obey.

I am told that if a person is drowning in the ocean and a lifeguard swims out for the rescue, the right thing for the drowning person to do is to quit struggling and simply submit to the grasp and the pulling of the lifeguard. If a person continues to struggle, the lifeguard may be unable to help and the person may drown just feet away from the qualified lifeguard.

Are you in a fight with life? Are you in a fight with God? OK. Stop. Submit, and let him rescue you and give you peace. In a few paragraphs, we will see the strong connection between submission and peace, but for now let us go back to our passage in 1 Peter. After the instruction to humble ourselves, we are told he will exalt us in due time.

There are some important lessons here. First, we see that it is the desire of the Lord to exalt us. He wants to bless us, to take care of us, and to meet our needs.

See how the Lord says this in the Old Testament.

> "I know the plans I have for you," declares the Lord, "plans to prosper you and not to harm you, plans to give you hope and a future."
>
> Jeremiah 29:11 NIV

Notice the verse teaches us that it is the Lord who will exalt us and that he will do this at the time he deems best. This is both a promise and a challenge. The promise is obvious. The challenge is difficult. It really goes back to humbling ourselves before him. We live in a world that is all about self-promotion and instant gratification. This is one of the reasons why stress is at epidemic levels. The challenge is to wait on the Lord and let him exalt us how and when he chooses.

Read this truth:

> Promotion cometh neither from the east, nor from the west, nor from the south. But God is the judge: He putteth down one, and setteth up another.
>
> Psalm 75:6–7 KJV

Can you do this? Can you quit fighting life and the Lord and wait on him to exalt you when it is time? The prophet Isaiah said, "Blessed are all those who wait for Him" (Isaiah 30:18).

So how does all of this help with stress? Now we get to the exciting part of the passage. Let us read it again.

> Humble yourselves, therefore, under the mighty hand of God so that at the proper time he may exalt you, casting all your anxieties on him, because he cares for you.
>
> 1 Peter 5:6-7

We are told to cast all our care upon him. The word *care* refers to the unavoidable stressors of life. Can you think of a few?

- Stressed about the uncertainty of your job's future…
- Stressed about the upcoming doctor's visit…
- Stressed about how tight the finances have become…
- Stressed about the 24/7 schedule of activities your family is involved in…

To cast these cares means to turn them over to God and let him worry about them. You may be thinking that is not so simple to do. Well, it becomes more simple the more we humble ourselves before him. It becomes more simple the more we learn to recognize he is ultimately in control and he cares for us, and he will exalt us in due time.

Can I give you the Noel-Dear-paraphrase of 1 Peter 5:6-7? Here it goes:

God assumes total responsibility for the life that is totally surrendered to him!

That is what these verses are telling us. If we will humble ourselves before him, then he will assume responsibility for our lives, our problems, and our future. He will take care of us in due time. We can rest assured of that.

Years ago, I made a sign that stated this important truth. I put the sign on my desk, and every time I would begin to be stressed over a problem or a person, I would read those words, think of 1 Peter 5:6-7, and smile.

A few years ago, I had moved into a new city and needed to rent a house until I could get settled in. When we moved in, we were given instructions about how to take care of the house and, in particular, the furnace. For the furnace, we were simply told to change the filter once a month. Well, one day, during our first winter in the home, the furnace broke. I knew I had followed the instructions I was given and had changed the filter faithfully. There was no problem there. So the broken furnace was not my problem. That is one of the nice things about renting a house. I called the property owner and asked him to have it repaired. He had a furnace repairperson come out and look at it, and they talked about whether it should be repaired or replaced, and what it was going to cost.

The name of the LORD is a strong tower; the righteous man runs into it and is safe.
—PROVERBS 18:10

How did that make me feel? Was I stressed over the furnace or the repair costs? No. Honestly, I did not really even care what it cost. I liked my property owner, and he was good to my family, so I hoped it would not cost him too much, but that was none of my business. It was a matter between him and the repairperson. I went on my merry way. I do not even recall what they did (repair or replace). All I know is my house was warm the next day. How nice it was to know it was someone else's problem.

Well, this passage tells us that if we humble ourselves before him, trust and submit, then it just is not our problem. God will deal with it. This truth has brought such a change in my life. When things happen now that would have caused me great stress a few years ago, I just ask this one question: Have I been trusting and submitting? If so, this is not my problem. It is his. That is the way he wants it to be.

In the Bible book of Colossians we are told, "Let the peace of Christ rule in your hearts" (Colossians 3:15). I am so glad I know how.

Look now at the last five words of the passage we are focusing on.

Because he cares for you.

You should memorize this. Preferably, memorize the entire passage and the Noel-Dear-paraphrase, but at least learn these five words. When stress begins to weigh on you, remember the one who is in control of it all, he cares for you!

Let me leave you with one more verse that encourages me when I am tempted to feel stress:

Peace I leave with you; my peace I give to you. Not as the world gives do I give to you. Let not your hearts be troubled, neither let them be afraid.

John 14:27

VINE DRESSING

1. What is the real cause of stress in your life?

2. In what areas of your life are you living outside of wise boundaries? Are you living outside the Lord's boundaries with your time? Your money? Your health? Your lifestyle choices?

3. What does it mean to "humble yourself under the hand of God?"

4. When you are living according to the Lord's wisdom and direction, and a problem arises, whose problem is it?

CHAPTER 15

SLAYING EMOTIONAL DRAGONS
DEPRESSION, PART 1

Caution: If you have flipped to back of this book to read about strategies for specific problems, then you are making a mistake. Without first understanding the material presented in the first ten chapters of this book, you will find this chapter confusing, controversial, and unsatisfying. Please read the first chapters first.

As we have already learned, the most effective way to eliminate depression from our lives is to grow and experience the fruit of the Spirit through abiding in Christ. That was the theme of the first half of this book. Sometimes, however, depression can be a particularly stubborn problem. When that is the case there can be a number of reasons including some medical issues, but what I have discovered both in counseling and in my study of God's Word, is that one very common denominator to this stubborn depression is simply sin. (By sin, I mean deliberately living outside the counsel of God as found in his word, the Bible.)

I am not suggesting depression is sin, or a depressed person is somehow a worse sinner than someone who is not depressed, but I am saying there is a connection between depression and sin that has not been properly dealt with.

Connections between Sin and Depression

So how could sin be a cause of depression? There are a number of reasons why. *First, sin poisons the soil from which we are trying to grow the fruit of the Spirit.* Joy will not grow in poisoned soil and there is no quicker way to poison soil than with sin. Imagine the effect of spreading weed killer all through your beautiful flower garden. It is likely the poison will kill not only the weeds, but also eliminate the flowers. This demonstrates why some people have such difficulty growing the fruit of the Spirit of joy.

Another reason sin contributes to depression is that sin separates us from the Lord. God hates sin. He hates it because it hurts us, and it dishonors him. Consequently, when we sin there is a real separation or rift that develops between him and us. What does that separation do? First, it prevents the Lord from helping and encouraging us, something he desires to do for his children and something we need for emotional and mental health. Secondly, it prevents us from hearing the wisdom of the Lord either through his Spirit or through his word. Have you ever noticed how stupid people become when they are engaged in sin? Have you wondered how a man could forfeit his wife and family for a few minutes of illicit pleasure? Have you ever wondered how a person could trade in his or her career, happiness, health, and family for a few too many bottles of beer? Sin makes us stupid because it takes us out of the range of hearing from our Lord.

Not only does sin cause depression because it separates us from the Lord, but also because it separates us from friends and family who could help and encourage us. Sometimes this separation is physical, meaning it takes us out of their presence, and sometimes it is emotional because it stops the free flow of honest sharing and encouragement. Maybe friends and family do not want to be around us because of the sin; maybe we do not want to be around them because of the sin; maybe the sin has driven us apart. Or maybe we have loved ones all around, but because of our secret sin and because of our guilty heart, we feel isolated and alone.

> *God designed us physically, mentally, and emotionally to live a certain way. When we live differently from that, which is the definition of sin, then it upsets the whole system.*

Another reason sin can cause depression is that God designed us physically, mentally, and emotionally to live a certain way. When we live differently from that, which is the definition of sin, then it upsets the whole system. Do you know the difference between diesel fuel and gasoline? Most of us do not know specifically, but we do know you should not put diesel fuel in a vehicle designed to run on gasoline or vice versa. If you take your carefully engineered, gasoline-consuming car and fill it up with diesel fuel the next time you are at the station, you will likely ruin your car. Why? It is because the car was designed to run on gasoline. Anything else will cause problems.

You and I are designed to live by the commands and principles found in God's word. When we go outside of those boundaries, we gum up our lives, and depression is just one of many consequences.

The final reason for sin causing depression is the discipline of the Lord. The Bible teaches us (Romans 12) that God loves us so much that he will bring discipline in our lives when we sin. He does this in order to get us back on the right track. This is a good thing. We have learned to discipline our children because we love them and want the best for them, and God does no less with us. So what are some of the ways the Lord disciplines us? One way is by removing our joy. In fact, when a Christian engages in sin, the Lord will sometimes remove all joy and usher in absolute misery. He wants to get our attention. He wants us to change before more serious and lasting consequences come our way.

You can never be completely free from the danger of depression as long as there is ongoing or unconfessed sin in your life.

Do you see how sin which has not been properly dealt with can bring depression? The truth is you can never be completely free from the danger of depression as long as there is ongoing or unconfessed sin in your life.

So in this chapter, we will learn about how to deal with ongoing sin. In the next chapter, we will learn to deal with unconfessed sin.

Ongoing Sin

We have already seen how ongoing sin can open us up for feelings of depression and we can probably think of some examples. What about the person who is lying and trying to keep up the pretense? That person feels the constant pressure of worrying if he or she is going to get caught. Have I told the same story to everyone? Do they suspect something? Am I about to be embarrassed or caught?

What about the person engaged in sexual sin? The guilt and the fear can invade every part of a person's life. Depression is a likely result.

We will see in a later chapter about how the sin of ongoing anger and bitterness can tear a person up emotionally. That bitterness can bubble up in a person's life in many different ways, and one of them is depression.

Notice what the Bible says:

> Let us throw off everything that hinders and the sin that so easily entangles. And let us run with perseverance the race marked out for us.
>
> Hebrews 12:1 NIV

For too many people, sin has tripped them up and they have fallen into the pit of depression. So let us learn how we can overcome sin because for every victory over sin, there are great benefits. Here are a few:

- God is honored. (Which, by the way, is the real purpose of our lives.)

- Our thankfulness for the sacrifice of Jesus Christ is displayed.

- There is eternal reward.

And to the point of this chapter and book, a little bit of depression is banished from our lives as the fruit of the Spirit of joy moves in.

Overcoming Sin

There is much to say about how to overcome sin. That could be a book or even a series of books all by itself. The Bible has a great deal to say about it, both for the why's and the how's. Let me just get you started by giving four broad steps. None of these are going to surprise you. None of this is rocket science. The power is not in the knowing; it is in the doing.

Step 1: Understand the seriousness of sin.

You will never be successful at removing sin until you realize its danger. As we have already seen in this chapter, sin causes a myriad of problems and the longer we engage in a particular sin, the worse those problems become and the harder it is to turn it around. Sin is deceptive in so many ways. Because of this, we always underestimate the cost of our sin, we misunderstand how quickly it spreads and we misjudge the depths of its roots in our life.

Do not be fooled. Playing with sin is like playing with radioactive waste. It always damages.

Step 2: Make a decision and make a change.

Many people will reflect on their sin and feel bad about it, and then just continue on. Others will have the best of intentions to change their ways, but those intentions will never turn into actions. If you want to overcome sin, you must make a decision and change.

Look at what the half-brother of Jesus wrote in the book of James.

> Put away all filthiness and rampant wickedness and receive with meekness the implanted word, which is able to save your souls.
>
> James 1:21

Filthiness and rampant wickedness are self-explanatory. The three key phrases in this verse are "put away," "all," and "implanted word."

"Put away" means to just take the sin out of your life and throw it away. It paints a picture of someone with filthy clothes, clothes covered in grease and grime and sweat, clothes you can smell from 100 yards away. The command is to take the clothes off and throw them away. If you are going to overcome ongoing sin, you are going to have to make a decision to remove it from your life.

One of the reasons many are so unsuccessful at overcoming sin is that they start out with a goal of only reducing their sin.

The word "all" tells us which sins we should remove from our lives. We should do this with *all* sin. One of the reasons many are so unsuccessful at overcoming sin is that they start out with a goal of only reducing their sin. That is not what the Scripture tells us to do. We must have a zero-tolerance policy. Now, will we really be sin free? Will we really completely overcome sin on this side of eternity? No, but the key to coming close enough to be able to eradicate depression with joy is to do *all* we can to lay aside *all* sin.

Sometimes people will tell me that their standard of "all sin" is 80% or 90%. Is that good enough? No! What if your doctor told you his goal was to remove 80-90% of the cancer in your colon? What if the bank told you they guaranteed they would keep 80-90% of your money safe? If you want success with this, you must strive to lay aside all sin.

The "implanted word" harkens back to what we learned in the first half of this book about the importance of getting God's word into our lives. If sin is allowed to remain, it will grow and bring the fruit of depression and destruction. However, if we plant God's word in our lives, and we water it daily through prayer and our daily appointment with the Lord, it will grow to give us the strength needed to overcome our ongoing sin.

Step 3: Employ some specific strategies to keep sin out of your life.

You know the areas of life where you are weakest. How can you have victory over these areas? Well, you need a plan.

Here are a few things that should be a part of every plan. *First, you should remove the source of temptation.* If you are tempted to look at or read pornography by having a computer and internet in the bedroom, then remove that temptation. If you are tempted to gossip when you talk on the phone with certain people, then stop taking their calls. You must figure out the greatest source of your temptation and then take drastic measures to remove that from your life.

The second thing that should be a part of your plan is to replace your sin with other things. Find something to focus your time and energy on so you are not sucked back into the old temptation.

Maybe a third element of your plan should be to write a consequence card. I carry a card in my wallet at all times where I have written the consequences I would face if I were guilty of sexual sin. I pull that out occasionally, and just read over it. It serves as a great reminder of why I need to avoid temptation in my life.

There are many strategies for keeping the sin you struggle with the most from resurfacing in your life. The important thing is that you have a plan for success. Do not just make a commitment and hope for the best. Put a plan together, and you will be much more likely to have this sin behind you forever.

Step 4: Get some help.

You do not have to do this alone. Find a friend you can trust to help hold you accountable. Tell that person about the weak areas in your struggle. Ask him or her to pray for you. Ask him or her to call you often and hold you accountable.

There are extremely important yet often overlooked instructions for this in the Bible:

> Confess your sins to one another and pray for one an-
> other, that you may be healed. The prayer of a righteous
> person has great power as it is working.
>
> James 5:16

Many people continue to struggle with the same sins and weaknesses repeatedly because they do not avail themselves of the power of the truth in this simple verse.

Another way to get help is always to be under the preaching and teaching of God's Word. God uses Bible teachers to help us apply God's word to our lives. This is one of the key elements to growing stronger in faith and closer to our Lord. Without regular intake of God's word through preaching and teaching, our efforts to overcome sin and bear the fruit of the Spirit will be anemic.

Finally, sometimes people need professional help. If you do all that we have discussed and you still struggle with certain sins, especially if they involve addictive behaviors, then you may need to seek professional help. Find a Christian counselor in your area. Call your pastor, and get his suggestions. Do not try to learn to live with sin. Strive to overcome it, and experience the joy of the Lord.

So with all of this, you can overcome your ongoing sin, and that is an essential step to knowing the joy that banishes depression.

VINE DRESSING

1. Sometimes there is a connection between sin and depression. How does that connection work? How can sin sometimes be the cause of depression?

2. What are the four steps to overcoming ongoing sin in your life?

CHAPTER 16

SLAYING EMOTIONAL DRAGONS
DEPRESSION, PART 2

Caution: If you have flipped to back of this book to read about strategies for specific problems, then you are making a mistake. Without first understanding the material presented in the first ten chapters of this book, you will find this chapter confusing, controversial, and unsatisfying. Please read the first chapters first.

In addition to ongoing sin, another category of sin that can lead to depression is unconfessed sin. This unconfessed sin can be something that has occurred recently or something that has occurred many years ago. It is sin that has simply not been properly dealt with before the Lord.

Unconfessed sin is very dangerous because, over time, it can negatively affect almost every part of our lives. John MacArthur, pastor of Grace Community Church in Sun

Valley, California and one of the leading Bible scholars in America today said, "Early in my pastoral ministry I noticed an interesting fact. Nearly all the personal problems that drive people to seek pastoral counsel are related in some way to the issue of forgiveness." And while there can be many issues involving forgiveness, and we will deal with some of those in the chapter on bitterness, one major issue is that of unconfessed sin.

Imagine all of your city's waste collecting in a giant cesspool and never being treated. After a while, that cesspool would stink up the entire city. People would get ill. Misery would rise. The mental image of that mess paints a good picture of what happens when our sin goes undealt with.

> He who covers his sin will not prosper, but whoever confesses and forsakes them will have mercy.
>
> Proverbs 28:13 NKJ

What if your husband decided one cold winter it was too much trouble to take the trash out to the street where the garbage service would pick it up? Instead of going to all of that trouble, what if he decided to just put it in your attic? For a while, that would probably work pretty well. The trash would be out of sight. Everyone would be happy. However, eventually this would begin to be a problem. How many days would it take before the stench of rotting leftovers in the attic worked its way down to the living areas of the house? How long before your entire attic would be infested with rats,

What if you just tossed your kitchen garbage in your attic for a few months?

maggots, and other unwanted living creatures? Eventually, the decaying trash would ruin the ceiling. The house would become unsafe and clean up would no longer be as simple as taking a few bags to the street.

That is what Proverbs 28:13 is talking about. We will never prosper; we will never grow the fruit of the Spirit; we will never experience true and lasting joy as long as we cover up our sins. Those sins may be out of sight, but their consequences have not been removed. In fact, the longer we cover up sins, the worse the consequences may become.

Look at these verses and see if this is a good description of depression.

> When I kept silent, my bones wasted away through my groaning all day long. For day and night your hand was heavy upon me; my strength was dried up as by the heat of summer.
>
> Psalm 32:3-4

The writer said he was silent before the Lord concerning his sin. The result of that silence was severe depression. He was suffering from physical pain and weakness. He was suffering from a great weight and burden on his heart and mind. He felt like his very life and vitality had dried up. Is there any hope? Yes there is. Look at the next verse in the Psalm.

> I acknowledged my sin to you, and I did not cover my iniquity; I said, "I will confess my transgressions to the Lord," and you forgave the iniquity of my sin.
>
> Psalm 32:5

We learn in this verse and in the rest of this Psalm that the writer then dealt with his sin before the Lord and found forgiveness and relief.

That is precisely what many people who are suffering from debilitating depression need to do. They need to take their unconfessed sin to the Lord and receive forgiveness and peace. Then, joy can return.

Unseen Damage

About every three to four months, I take my car to the mechanic and get him to change the oil. Part of me thinks this is a waste of time and money. I have never seen the oil in my current car. The old oil does not seem to be causing any problems I am aware of. Why go to the trouble? Why go to the expense?

It is because whether I can see it or hear it or not, the old oil is slowly but surely damaging my engine. If I never change it, I will have problems, very expensive problems. In fact, the car may run fine until one day it just seizes up without warning. The engine could be destroyed. The same is true with our sin and us. If we do not regularly go before the Lord and deal with our sin, the old sin will damage our life. We may not see the damage early on. We may be unaware of the danger. Nevertheless, one day we will pay a price. One day we will lose our joy because of the un-dealt with sin.

So what is the solution? What can we do? What should we do?

Some people might argue at this point that there is no need to deal with sin in our past because as believers we have already been forgiven by the Lord. It is true that the forgiveness of the Lord extends to all sins his children have been guilty of or will one day be guilty of. We should thank the Lord for that truth, but let us not forget the Bible still commands us to confess our sins to him. The Bible even gives a picture of this confession in what is commonly called the Lord's Prayer (see Matthew 6:12).

So what is the point of dealing with our sin before the Lord if it has already been forgiven? While technically, forgiveness is not needed, there is a broken fellowship with the Lord that does need to be mended.

When we sin, our fellowship with God is broken. God forgives us, but we do not enjoy the full benefits of that forgiveness until the fellowship is restored. Let me illustrate with a story.

A Modern Day Parable

Once upon a time, there were two children ages ten and twelve visiting their grandmother who lived out in the country. Playing outside, the boy threw a rock at a bird in his grandmother's flower garden only to miss the bird and hit a ceramic figurine his grandmother had placed in the center of the garden. The figurine shattered. The boy knew he was in trouble when he turned around and saw his older sister staring right at him. He ran to his sister and begged her not to tell their grandmother. The sister agreed as long as the boy did all her chores for the week. The brother was not thrilled, but had no choice. He agreed.

Later that night, after dinner, the grandmother told the girl it was her turn to clean the table and wash the dishes. She smiled and said, "Grandmother, I think my brother would love to do that for me." She smiled at her brother who promptly jumped up and began to take care of the dishes.

The next morning, the grandmother told the daughter to sweep off the back porch since they were expecting guests soon. The girl just smiled and said, "My brother loves to sweep. He won't mind doing it." The brother immediately began to sweep.

This pattern continued for a few days until eventually the boy broke down and shouted, "I can't do this anymore." The grandmother asked what was going on, and the boy told the whole story of how he had broken the figurine with a rock and made the deal with his sister. He expressed to his grandmother how sorry he was for throwing the stone and breaking the figurine. As he was explaining and apologizing, his grandmother began to smile. She said, "Son, I was standing at the window when you threw the rock and broke the figurine. I was disappointed, but I forgave you immediately. You never had to hide this, and you never had to make that deal with your sister." She hugged her grandson, and it was all over.

The Lesson

While the boy had been forgiven immediately, because he did not go and confess to his grandmother, he suffered for days as if he had not been forgiven. *He only began to enjoy all of the benefits of forgiveness when he confessed.* The same thing is true in our relationship and fellowship with the Lord. We have already been forgiven, but confession is still needed to restore our walk and fellowship with the Lord and to experience the free flow of his joy in our life again.

So how do we confess? How do we deal with our past sin before the Lord? The simplest answer is found in a command the Bible gives to believers:

> If we confess our sins, he is faithful and just to forgive us our sins and to cleanse us from all unrighteousness.
>
> 1 John 1:9

How To Confess

There are four parts to confession. I am going to make them all start with the letter "A" so they are easily remembered.

Part 1: Agree

The first part of confession is agreeing with the Lord that what we have done is sin. The Greek word for "confess" means to say the same thing. Too often in our culture, we try to excuse what the Bible clearly calls sin by assigning softer labels to it. We call our offenses mistakes or habits. We label them as diseases or syndromes. We call our sin a weakness or a propensity. The truth is, it is sin. We should say so and agree with the Lord that it was wrong and should never have occurred.

Part 2: Appreciate

The second thing we must do is to have some appreciation of the Lord's role in our forgiveness. Forgiveness is not as simple as a police officer saying he will give us a warning instead of a ticket. When you speed, that is not a personal offense against the police officer, and the police officer does not pay for the ticket he did not give to you. No, the police officer just ignores the offense.

All sin is an offense against the Lord.

All sin, however, is an offense against the Lord. When you sin, you may sin against some person in your life, but in a real sense, you have also sinned against God. Also, for God to forgive sin, he removes the penalty from your life and places it on someone else. That someone else is his son, Jesus Christ. That is what the cross is all about: Jesus paying the price for your guilt and sin.

Read this powerful verse:

> God made Christ, who never sinned, to be the offering for our sin [to pay the price for our sin], so that we could be made right with God through Christ.
>
> 2 Corinthians 5:21 NLT

So a part of confession is remembering and appreciating that forgiveness is a very costly thing. God chose to make this possible and to pay for it out of his love. It should never be taken lightly.

Part 3: Ask

The next part of confession is the asking. This is simple, but it is important. We must express our sorrow for the sin and ask the Lord to restore our broken fellowship. This is such an important thing if we really desire to know, or know again, the joy of the Lord.

Part 4: Apply

The last part of confession is application. If this is an ongoing sin, we must, with the Lord's help, make a change. Look back to the previous chapter for help on making this change effective.

It Is Time To Be Free

What now? It is important that you do not wallow around in your sin once you have repented and confessed. You are forgiven! There is no condemnation for you (Romans 8:1).

One of the most well-known parables in the Bible is the story of the prodigal son. This son disrespected his father, took his father's money, violated his father's rules, and abandoned his father's house. Eventually, the son returned. As he returned, he dreaded and feared what the reaction of his father might be. When his father saw him coming down the road, he ran to meet him. He hugged and forgave him. Then he threw a party. So where did the son go during the party?

Did he sit in his room? Was he sent to the fields to work? No. He was at the party! He was forgiven! This was not time for gloom. This was time for rejoicing.

Once you have dealt with your sin before the Lord, then step out of your guilt. You are a child of the King. There is no longer any guilt on your account. Rejoice in the Lord.

I have learned through counseling with a number of people who are depressed because of past sins in their lives that sometimes people do not want to rejoice. Sometimes they feel so bad because of what they have done that they think it would be wrong to feel good again. In some sense, they like their depression because to them it is penance or payback for their sin. If that is you, please understand this: Your forgiveness is real. Jesus really did pay for your sin. No further debt is owed by you or anyone else. There should be no shame in feeling the release of forgiveness. Celebrate your freedom and Christ's sacrifice and love by embracing the joy of the Lord!

Let this Psalm encourage you.

> He does not deal with us according to our sins, nor repay us according to our iniquities. For as high as the heavens are above the earth, so great is his steadfast love toward those who fear him; as far as the east is from the west, so far does he remove our transgressions from us.
>
> Psalm 103:10-12

The Lord desires to replace your depression with joy. John 10:10 says in part, "I came that they may have life and have it abundantly."

He is simply waiting for us to deal with our past sins by confessing them to him.

I am reminded of the story of the sin of Adam and Eve. After their sin, the Bible says God the Father chose to walk through the garden to see them. What do you think the Father was coming to do? Was he just coming to destroy them? To mete out some terrible punishment? No. He could have done that without coming to walk among them. I believe the Father was coming to begin to restore the broken relationship. I believe the Father came in love.

The Father is still walking around looking to show love and kindness to his children who are hidden in sin. Are you ready to come clean and be made clean?

VINE DRESSING

1. Why is it always a bad idea to just cover up past sins?

2. What is the connection between depression and old sins that have never been dealt with?

3. If our sins have been forgiven, what is the benefit in confessing them individually before the Lord?

4. What are the four A's of how-to confess our sin?

5. What sins are hidden and un-dealt with in your life? What is your plan to put these to rest once and for all?

CHAPTER 17

SLAYING EMOTIONAL DRAGONS
ANGER

Caution: If you have flipped to back of this book to read about strategies for specific problems, then you are making a mistake. Without first understanding the material presented in the first ten chapters of this book, you will find this chapter confusing, controversial, and unsatisfying. Please read the first chapters first.

Another dragon that endangers our emotional health and vitality is anger. Even with the fruit of the Spirit growing in a person's life, anger can bring misery and destruction. So what should we do if we find ourselves angry?

It helps to begin with an understanding of the seriousness of anger. What are the potential consequences of our anger? Let us make a list.

- Anger can cause you to say things you later regret.

- Anger can cause you to say or do things that jeopardize your marriage or other key relationships.

- Anger can lead to all kinds of crimes like child abuse, assault, or even murder.

- Anger can split a family, divide friends, or even ruin churches.

- Anger can make holes in walls.

- Anger can put you in the unemployment line.

- Anger often leads to embarrassment and regret.

- Anger weakens the immune system, spikes blood pressure, aggravates ulcers, and ruins sleep.

Anger makes you stupid. You know that to be true. When a person becomes angry, his or her IQ drops twenty points. You witness that person saying and doing things that are, for lack of a better word, stupid. They say and do things they would never say or do under normal circumstances.

There is a righteous anger, a good and appropriate anger, but that is not the kind of anger that has prompted you to read this chapter. You have a righteous anger when you oppose things that anger the Lord. Righteous anger never leads to sin. It never leads to regret. It never leads to an out-of-control spirit. If we are angry because we have been hurt or offended; if our temper and our words are being driven by our anger; if anger is taking control of our thoughts, then it is the dangerous kind, and it will lead to a bad place if it is not brought quickly under control.

The Bible is filled with warnings about the dangers of anger. (It is interesting that the word anger is found within the word danger. That should serve as a helpful reminder of the jeopardy anger brings.) Look at some of these verses.

> Better to dwell in the wilderness, Than with a contentious and angry woman.
>
> Proverbs 21:19 NKJ

This verse reminds us that anger can drive a wedge between a husband and wife.

> Make no friendship with a man given to anger, nor go with a wrathful man.
>
> Proverbs 22:24

Here we learn that when you are angry, your anger hurts not only you, but also those who are friends with you and those who are around you. Anger robs some of the joy from their lives too.

> A man of great wrath will pay the penalty, for if you deliver him, you will only have to do it again.
>
> Proverbs 19:19 and

A man of great wrath is the same as a man of great anger. The verse tells us that he will suffer because of his anger and even if he is rescued, he will likely just get angry again and suffer again. Here we learn that a problem with anger can be very hard to overcome if it is not taken seriously.

> Don't sin by letting anger control you. Don't let the sun go down while you are still angry, for anger gives a foothold to the devil.
>
> Ephesians 4:26–27 NLT

This is a verse we will study more closely later in this chapter, but notice the consequence given in the last few words. When we are angry, we allow the devil to get a foothold in our life. Because of this, our anger can lead to so many more sins. It can lead to foolish words, foolish decisions, and foolish actions. Therefore, anger is danger. So what should we do to overcome it?

Overcoming Anger

The first step is to act without delay. Anger is like a fire in your house. The longer you wait to do something about it the more damage it will do and the harder it will be to stop. When Jesus talked about anger in his famous "Sermon on the Mount," he stressed the importance of dealing with your adversary, or the source of your anger, quickly.

Let us look again at the verse from Ephesians 4.

> Don't sin by letting anger control you. Don't let the sun go down while you are still angry, for anger gives a foothold to the devil.
>
> Ephesians 4:26-27 NLT

If you let anger exist in your heart and mind for even twenty-four hours, you have not dealt with it quickly enough. So what should you do? We will learn some steps to take through the remainder of this chapter but the first lesson to learn is the worst thing you can do is to do nothing.

Some people, when angry, will just sit, stew, and simmer. Those people will suffer the worst effects of anger. In fact, the Bible teaches that dealing with anger is more important than worship (Matthew 5:24) and sleep (Ephesians 4:26). So make plans to deal quickly with your anger.

> *Be not quick in your spirit to become angry, for anger lodges in the heart of fools.*
> —ECC. 7:9

Some people might say there is some anger that simply cannot be dealt with in one twenty-four hour period, and those people would be right in a sense. Your anger may not be able to be resolved before the sun sets, but I believe the lesson this passage is teaching is that you should start to resolve your anger before the sun goes down. Until you begin to resolve the issue, the anger is going to continue to damage you. Healing should at least begin on day one.

Waiting on God

The next item on your anger management to-do list should be to "let God" or "wait on God." One of the reasons we embrace anger is because we believe we are bringing justice to the situation. We want to make a point. We want to make the offending party suffer or pay. If you find those kinds of thoughts running through your mind, then know this: That is not your job!

Read how the Bible says this.

> Do not take revenge, my dear friends, but leave room
> for God's wrath, for it is written: "It is mine to avenge;
> I will repay," says the Lord.
>
> Romans 12:19 NIV

The Lord promises he will take care of all injustices in the right way and at the right time. We should trust him to do so.

In fact, this is a self-benefiting command. Think about it. When you seek to pay someone back for his or her wrong, the first thing you do is reopen the wound. You undo all of the healing you have experienced over time. Secondly, you end up causing pain, not just for the one your payback is focused on but also on yourself. Third, you have pushed God out of the process. You have prevented him from fighting on your behalf.

Stop being angry! Turn from your rage! Do not lose your temper—it only leads to harm.
—Psalm 37:8

I think about the Old Testament account of Joseph and his brothers. Joseph's brothers had mistreated him, beat him, and sold him as a slave into a foreign culture. Fast forward a bunch of years and it turns out Joseph became the second highest ruler in the most powerful nation on earth, and his brothers found themselves at his mercy. When they went to him to beg him not to punish them for their hateful crimes against him, Joseph said this, "Do not be afraid, for am I in the place of God" (Genesis 50:19)?

Joseph did not reopen the old wounds. He did not cause some big problem that further separated the family. He simply left it in God's hands. That is a very good pattern to follow.

Remember Grace

What to do next? Remember the grace of the Lord.

We will learn more about the power of this in the next chapter, but let me say here that when anger begins to boil in your heart, it is essential that you remember how good the Lord has been to you. Remember how the Lord has forgiven you of some pretty serious offenses. Think about all of the times he has bailed you out and rescued you from terrible decisions. In light of this grace, you will find your anger will shrink.

I can think right now of times when I have listened to someone spew vitriol and stupidity with their words, and I wanted to lash out at them with my own words and put them in their place. Then the Lord reminded me of some of the foolish words I have said in my past and how he has forgiven me, and my anger diminished.

Read this proverb.

> Good sense makes one slow to anger, and it is his glory to overlook an offense.
>
> Proverbs 19:11

What do we learn from this? A wise man will be slow to get angry and his glory, which means the very best thing about him, is that he can overlook a transgression. He can, in light of all of his own sin and the forgiveness he has received, let things go.

Speak Softly

The next part of this strategy to abate anger is to speak softly.

Anger is like a fire, and your lips are like gasoline. When you combine these two things, you can easily have an explosion.

Look at some of these Bible truths:

> A soft answer turns away wrath, but a harsh word stirs up anger.
>
> Proverbs 15:1

According to this verse, one thing reduces anger and another thing stirs it up. Do you see the two?

> You must all be quick to listen, slow to speak, and slow to get angry. Human anger does not produce the righteousness God desires.
>
> James 1:19–20 NLT

Here we are reminded that it is those who are quick to speak who aggravate anger and create unrighteousness.

There is another key element for the control of anger and we will learn that in the next chapter, but let me outline what we have learned so far. Anger is dangerous, physically, emotionally, and spiritually. The longer we allow anger to fester in our lives, the more dangerous it becomes. The first strategy to battle anger is to learn to wait on the Lord to move, to remember the Lord's forgiveness in our lives when we have sinned, and to be careful to control our speech.

VINE DRESSING

1. What are some of the things unchecked anger can lead to? What negative things have you seen anger bring into a person's life?

2. What does the Bible mean when it says, "Don't let the sun go down on your anger?"

3. Whose responsibility is it to mete out justice? Whose job is it to avenge or take revenge?

4. Why do we really have no ground to stand on when we are angry? What has the Lord done for us that should preclude our anger?

CHAPTER 18

SLAYING EMOTIONAL DRAGONS
BITTERNESS

Caution: If you have flipped to back of this book to read about strategies for specific problems, then you are making a mistake. Without first understanding the material presented in the first ten chapters of this book, you will find this chapter confusing, controversial, and unsatisfying. Please read the first chapters first.

Do you know what bitterness looks like? It looks like a sour attitude, an angry and caustic spirit, and a contagious misery. We all know people who are infected with bitterness and most of us have struggled with this debilitating outlook and attitude more than once in our own lives. So what is the big deal with bitterness? Why does it hurt people so much? Why is it so hard to get rid of? How do people fall into this pit of knives?

Let us see what we can learn.

First, why is it so dangerous? It is dangerous because it can literally ruin your life. It is said, bitterness is like an acid that destroys its own container. The Bible calls bitterness a poison (Acts 8:23). Little by little, bitterness can rob a person of their joy, their hope, their relationships, and their future. Moreover, all of this can happen without the bitter person ever realizing the progression.

On top of that, bitterness is really hard to self-diagnose. Most bitter people have no idea they are bitter. You may have noticed there are no books on how to overcome bit-

Time heals some wounds, but it only exacerbates bitterness.

terness. That is not because there is not a need. There is an incredible need, but the people who would need to read the books do not know they are bitter. The Bible says bitterness is a root sin. One quality of a root is that it is buried. It is unseen. Roots cause weeds to grow, but you ordinarily never see the root. You only see the weeds. Bitterness causes many problems, but often, especially for the bitter person, the root of the problem is not seen. Bitterness is the best-camouflaged problem people have.

Even if you try to confront a bitter person and point out his bitterness, he will often deny it. Immediately he will begin to tell you all of the valid reasons he has to be mad. He will point to some situation or some person and explain why his anger is justified. And while all of that might be true, he misses the point: He is bitter, and he is suffering, and his situation is going to get worse if he does not acknowledge and deal with his bitterness.

Why is this always the case? It is because time is the enemy of the person suffering from bitterness. Time does heal *some* wounds. For instance, if you are grieving over a very difficult loss, time will likely make your grief at least a little lighter. However, with bitterness, time only makes it worse. Bitterness is like cancer. The longer it remains untreated in your body the more rooted it will become, the more parts of your body it will attack, and the more difficult it will be to treat.

Bitterness and Illness

Speaking of illnesses, bitterness can make you sick. Not only does it poison your spirit, it can poison your body. Go online and count the number of illnesses associated with stress, anxiety and depression and multiply all of that by a factor of ten and you may get close to the possible physical effects of bitterness. I once heard someone correctly say, "You can be sick and not be bitter, but you cannot be bitter for long and not be sick."

But maybe the most tragic effect of bitterness is that it hurts others. Bitterness is not a solo affliction. If you are bitter, then you will be miserable, and so will the people who are around you. Bitterness can be contagious.

The Bible teaches that when a person allows a root of bitterness to find its way into his life, consequently, many others will be defiled or corrupted (Hebrews 12:15). None of us want to diminish or destroy our own lives, but the stakes are even higher when we realize we could be doing the same to those we care about the most.

The Beginning of Bitterness

So what causes the plight of bitterness? There are many things that can add to the misery of bitterness and aggravate its pain, but the genesis of the problem is anger and specifically the anger that comes from a refusal to forgive. When someone sins against you, and they will, you have a choice. You can forgive that person for their offense, or you can take a step toward the pit of bitterness.

Jesus gives us an incredibly insightful parable to help us see how bitterness begins, why it is so painful (and painful for so long), and even how to overcome it. There are three parts to this story. Look at part one.

> Peter came to Jesus and asked, "Lord, how many times shall I forgive my brother or sister who sins against me? Up to seven times?"
>
> Jesus answered, "I tell you, not seven times, but seventy-seven times. Therefore, the kingdom of heaven is like a king who wanted to settle accounts with his servants. As he began the settlement, a man who owed him ten thousand bags of gold was brought to him. Since he was not able to pay, the master ordered that he and his wife and his children and all that he had be sold to repay the debt. At this the servant fell on his knees before him. 'Be patient with me,' he begged, 'and I will pay back everything.' The servant's master took pity on him, canceled the debt and let him go."
>
> Matthew 18:21–27 NIV

The parable is given in response to a question about how often a person should forgive. The custom of the day among many of the religious people was to limit forgiveness to three times. Jesus said forgiveness should have no limit and then he gives the parable we have begun to read.

In the parable, there are three main characters. We see the first two in this part, the king and the servant. The king called in the servant to demand he pay his debt. As it turns out his debt was so large, he could never repay. The servant then begged the king for mercy and to everyone's surprise, the king forgave the debt. What a wonderful act of kindness. I wonder how the servant must have felt. He had to have been happy. I wonder if he shouted. I wonder if he danced. I wonder if he kissed the guard who a few minutes earlier was about to throw him into debtor's prison.

So the forgiven servant walks, or skips, out of the palace, and here begins the second part of the story. Brace yourself for a dramatic shift.

> But when that servant went out, he found one of his
> fellow servants who owed him a hundred silver coins.
> He grabbed him and began to choke him. "Pay back
> what you owe me!" he demanded. His fellow servant
> fell to his knees and begged him, "Be patient with me,
> and I will pay it back." But he refused. Instead, he went
> off and had the man thrown into prison until he could
> pay the debt.
>
> Matthew 18:28–30 NIV

He did what? So the servant who had been forgiven a debt of ten thousand bags of gold could not find the kindness in his heart to forgive his fellow servant a hundred silver coins? That is crazy. What was he thinking? The problem is that he was not thinking. He did not make any connection between what he had been forgiven and what others owed him. This is a critical error; one that will cost him dearly. Remember this missed connection; we will see in a few paragraphs that this is the key to bitterness and its resolution.

The Rest of the Story

When the other servants saw what had happened, they were outraged and went and told their master everything that had happened. Then the master called the servant in. "You wicked servant," he said, "I canceled all that debt of yours because you begged me to. Shouldn't you have had mercy on your fellow servant just as I had on you?" In anger his master handed him over to the jailers to be tortured, until he should pay back all he owed. This is how my heavenly Father will treat each of you unless you forgive your brother or sister from your heart.

Matthew 18:31–35 NIV

It serves him right! Right? Because of his refusal to forgive, in light of the incredible forgiveness he had received, the servant was arrested and thrown into prison and tortured indefinitely.

Then Jesus adds a word of explanation at the end of the story. He says this will be the condition of every person who refuses to forgive when someone offends them.

Do you see who the real characters are in this parable? The king represents God, the heavenly Father. The first servant represents you and me, who have been forgiven by God more than we could ever have repaid. The fellow servant represents the person who has hurt or offended us. He represents the person we are unwilling to forgive. The torture chamber? That represents the life of bitterness.

Now do you understand why some people are caught in the trap of bitterness? Do you understand why it is so hard to escape from bitterness? What should a person do? How can this be overcome?

The key step in overcoming bitterness is to remember we have been forgiven. That was the problem of the servant in the parable. He had lost sight of the incredible forgiveness he had received. Why should I forgive those who may hurt or offend me? Because the Holy Father in Heaven has forgiven me much more than I am being asked to forgive the offending party in my life. If for no other reason than gratitude for my forgiveness, I should be ready and willing to forgive.

When we read this parable, we are very quick to condemn this servant for his foolish, inconsiderate actions. We call him cruel and unreasonable. The reason we say these things is that in the parable we see the two debts side by side. It is easy for us to compare the two and come quickly to our conclusion about the absurdity of the servant's actions. The problem in real life is that we do not often have this perspective. We see the forgiveness we have received from the Lord for our sins and the need for forgiveness for those who have hurt us as completely separate things. If we can broaden our perspective and see those things in the same picture, then it will be much easier to extend forgiveness and avoid bitterness.

How To Forgive

So how do we extend forgiveness? How can I truly forgive someone who has hurt me?

When an offense occurs, then a debt is created. If someone steals $100 from you, now there is a $100 debt. If someone backs into your car and dents in your left back fender, then there is a debt in the amount of whatever it will take to repair the fender. If someone hurts you physically or emotionally, then there is a debt. It is much harder to quantify or measure that kind of debt, but it is a debt nonetheless.

Therefore, forgiveness happens when you decide not to charge that debt to the offending person's account. If someone backs into my car and causes $1,000 in damage, for me to forgive them would be for me to say, "Don't worry about the $1,000. I will pay it. You are forgiven."

If someone slanders me with their words such that I am embarrassed and I maybe even lose some friends or perhaps my job, then a debt has been created. Not necessarily a financial debt, but a debt of pain and disappointment. For me to forgive would involve deciding that I would not charge the offense to them. Forgiveness means that I say, "You do not owe me anything for what you did and what followed. I will take the pain on myself. I do not charge it to your account. I will not bring it up again either in my mind or especially in my words when I see or hear of you."

That might seem like a very hard or impossible thing to do, but remember, that is what the heavenly Father did for you. He took the debt created by your willful sins and instead of charging you with it; he allowed his Son, Jesus Christ, to pay the price on the cross. Being a child of God means exactly that. He has not charged our guilt to us. We are in the same boat as the servant in the parable who had been forgiven so much by the king. Once we received the forgiveness of God, we forfeited for all time, our right to hold sin against anyone again.

Forgiving and Forgetting

At this point in thinking through how to forgive, people will often say, "I can't forgive because I just can't forget. In fact, I will never forget what he did to me."

This kind of sentiment points out a giant myth about forgiveness. People think forgiving somehow equates to forgetting. That is not true. Quit beating yourself up because you cannot forget. To forgive means you choose not to bring it up again. It means you do not rehearse it in your mind. It means you do not mention it in a future argument. Forgiving is not forgetting; it is choosing not to actively try to remember.

Motivations

Can remembering the fact that you have been forgiven give you the strength to let things go? It is the first step. There is another motivation that will help. Not only do we need to remember we have been forgiven, but we need to remember the cost of refusing to forgive.

In the parable Jesus told, what happened to the servant who refused to forgive? His refusal led to his torture! You might ask, "Would God really do that?" Well, look around. Do you know people whose lives are tortured because of bitterness?

Another Modern Day Parable

Near where I live, the state has built a new four-lane road that cuts through what was mostly farmland to connect two cities together. I travel that road often. It really cuts down on my travel time, and makes for a safer ride to the big city. Every time I go down that road, though, I notice a house that is very close to the fence alongside the road. I notice this house because of the epitaph that has been spray painted on the wall facing the road. I will not repeat the imperative here, but it makes a derogatory statement about the Ohio Department of Transportation.

Apparently, the owner of the house, who it appears has now abandoned the house, feels that he or she was wrongly treated by the road department. Is that the case? Was he mistreated? I have no idea. Perhaps he was. Perhaps he was badly mistreated. That is not the point now. The point now is that it seems he is allowing what happened a couple of years ago to destroy his happiness today.

I do not know the person or his current demeanor, but I have counseled with enough people to make a good guess. I imagine that house and that epitaph stand as monuments to his anger and his bitterness. Sure, he perhaps lost his yard when the road came through, maybe he lost a few thousand dollars in unreimbursed depreciation on his property, but now he has lost much more. He could not stop the transportation department from taking his property, but he can stop them from taking his life if he will only forgive. Daily, he is losing his opportunity for joy. He is losing his life! Every time I see that house, I want to find the owner and say, "OK. You have made your point. You were ripped off. Now drop it. Forgive. Enjoy life!" I do not know the details of the financial payment and whether it fairly compensated him for his loss, but I do know this: What he has likely voluntarily forfeited in lost joy is much more than what they involuntarily took from him in property value.

So how can we forgive and escape from the bitterness that can destroy our lives? There are four steps.

- Ask for God's help. (He has done this before. He will help you if you ask him to.)

- Transfer the debt the offending party owes to your own account. (Do not charge them any longer.)

- Refuse to remember or rehearse the offense in your mind. (Every time it comes up, refuse to ponder on it.)

- Communicate the forgiveness. (Begin to have some closure by expressing to the offender that you have forgiven him or her. If he knew about the anger, then he should know about the forgiveness.)

We must make it a high priority to remove any bitter root from our lives. Find a way, any way, quickly, before it is too late.

Read the warning about bitterness the Bible gives in the book of Hebrews:

> Strive for peace with everyone, and for the holiness without which no one will see the Lord. See to it that no one fails to obtain the grace of God; that no "root of bitterness" springs up and causes trouble, and by it many become defiled;
>
> Hebrews 12:14-15

VINE DRESSING

1. What does it mean that the Bible calls bitterness a "root sin?"

2. Is bitterness a sin that only hurts the guilty person or does it impact all of those around the guilty person? How serious does this make the issue of bitterness?

3. What is the primary cause of bitterness?

4. The man in the parable who was forgiven of such a great debt committed a terrible sin. What was his sin? What were the consequences of his sin?

5. What does it really mean to forgive someone?

6. Do we have to forget in order to forgive?

7. What are the practical steps in extending forgiveness to someone who has hurt you?

A Final Note...

Thank you for reading this book. The information you have read has gone through many revisions through the years as I have studied God's word further and as I have had more and more interactions with people seeking recovery from mental and emotional illnesses. I hope the updates can continue and that this material can become even more helpful.

I would very much appreciate your feedback and your reports of struggles and victories. To share your story, visit www.IlluminatingTheDarkness.com or email NoelDear@ IlluminatingTheDarkness.com.

Noel Dear